Am I the Only One Here With Faded Genes?

Am I the Only One Here With Faded Genes?

MARIE CHAPIAN

BETHANY HOUSE PUBLISHERS
MINNEAPOLIS, MINNESOTA 55438
A Division of Bethany Fellowship, Inc.

Photos by Liza Chapian.

We wish to thank the young people of Calvary Chapel, Encinitas, California, whose photos appear on the pages of this book.

Published by Bethany House Publishers
A Division of Bethany Fellowship, Inc.
6820 Auto Club Road, Minneapolis, Minnesota 55438

Printed in the United States of America

Library of Congress Cataloging-in-Publication Data

Chapian, Marie.
    Am I the only one here with faded genes?

    Summary: Devotionals, anecdotes, and prayers for teenagers on such issues as peer pressure, self-confidence, relationships, depression, anxiety, anger, and fear of failure.
    1. Youth—Prayer-books and devotions—English.
[1. Prayer books and devotions. 2. Christian life]
I. Title.
BV4850.C48   1987   242'.63   87-11611
ISBN 0-87123-945-0 (pbk.)

To every teen who has ever called out to God
and wondered when He'd answer . . .

With thanks
to my best friends
and truest pals,
the teenagers I live with.

Christa and Liza.

MARIE CHAPIAN, Ph.D., is known around the world as an author and speaker. She also is a Christian counselor and a familiar personality to radio and TV audiences. She has written 20 books with translations in eleven languages.

Preface

To my knowledge, this is a first. No writer I have come across yet has unlocked specifically for teens the treasure available to those who let the truth change their thinking patterns. Moreover, none has until now woven devotional meditations together with an emphasis on "truth in the inward parts." In the language of youth and with powerful application to everyday life, the author guides teens to true freedom—in thought, word and action.

No other writer could do it as well as Marie Chapian. Working with Marie on our book *Telling Yourself the Truth* reinforced what years of friendship and professional association had already shown me: She has an almost uncanny ability to grasp abstract ideas and to translate them into clear, sparkling, concrete, life-related concepts on paper.

Marie has done that again in this devotional book for teens. I predict that, through it, the lives of many young people will be revolutionized!

William Backus, Ph.D.
Forest Lake, Minnesota

Contents

10

Introduction

I heard a minister tell about being on the beach one day and spotting a young man who looked like he was drowning. The pastor raced into the water with a Boogie board, paddled to the victim and saved his life. Ecstatic at having saved him from drowning, the minister was puzzled when the young man, about seventeen, quickly tried to get away.

"What's the matter?" his rescuer questioned.

"I don't want my friends to know I was drowning," he muttered. "That's why I didn't yell for help—please don't tell them."

That may sound like incredible thinking, but consider your own life. Maybe, right now, you feel as if you're drowning in problems: Your parents just shortened your weekend curfew, a whole grade point was lopped off your paper because it was late, your face is breaking out *again*, and your best friend is taking *her* to a movie. It's okay to admit you're going under and need help.

It's time to start telling yourself the truth. First, you're *not* the only person with "faded genes"—nobody has a perfect family, perfect friends, perfect body, or perfect anything. Second, admitting your frustration and discouragement means you're on the way to help, not to un-

11

bearable shame and unhappiness. You can, instead, see yourself as God sees you: A person of unmeasured worth who can bring joy to your heavenly Father, your family and friends, (even your teachers!) and yourself.

The genes you have inherited—good, bad or indifferent—do not decide your failure or success in life. Jesus said to His disciples (many of them teenagers), "Do not worry about your life . . . who of you by worrying can add a single hour to his life? Since you cannot do this very little thing, why do you worry about the rest?" This book will show you *how to not worry* about your problems and *how to become and enjoy* the person God wants you to be.

Your friend,
Marie Chapian

Chapter 1

Born to Win

I learned recently that in tattoo parlors there is a tattoo a person can have put on his body reading, BORN TO LOSE. Now, can you imagine permanently imprinting such a lie on your body and living with it for the rest of your life?

A man who runs a tattoo parlor says this in explanation of such a gross and ugly defilement of human value: "First the picture is tattooed on the mind. Then on the body."

What have you tattooed on your mind today? Would you wear those words on your body? How would you like to go to school with a big tattoo on your chest reading, I'M TOO FAT TO WEAR MY JEANS, or some other negative thing you're always telling yourself?

One teenage boy I know has

The Lord your God will set you high above all the nations on earth. All these blessings will come upon you and accompany you if you obey the Lord your God.

Deuteronomy 28:1, 2

13

tattooed on his mind, I'M TOO SKINNY. He might as well wear those words across his forehead. He even *acts* skinny. Another boy I know has I'M TOO SHORT tattooed on his mind.

What's *your* tattoo?

If the first words you spoke every morning were tattooed on your body, what would they be? How about: "Hello, world, it's me, a great person, and Jesus loves me!"

Just imagine all the thoughts you have first thing in the morning being permanently tattooed on your body. Could you really live with, I HATE THIS TOOTHPASTE,

14

for the rest of your life? How about, GOD LOVES ME, instead?

Remember, tattoos are on the heart first, then in the mind, then on the body. You think first. Then you act. You *are* what you think, and you *do* what you think about. Plant these words in your mind right now: *I am born to win!* Say it out loud.

You were born to win and that's the truth. "The Lord your God will set you high above all the nations on earth. All these blessings will come upon you and accompany you if you obey the Lord your God." Now, do these words sound like threats to a loser?

If you are born again, you are swept clean by the healing, forgiving love of your Savior, Jesus. You're filled with the Holy Spirit, *God's* spirit. God is no loser and He doesn't create losers. He creates winners and breathes creative, joyful power into you. Tell yourself at least ten times every day, *"I'm born to win!"*

TODAY

Remove the negative tattoos from your mind and replace them with the blazing, powerful *truth*. You were born to please God and be His delight. You are a winner. Born to win. Winners don't tattoo their bodies with dumb sayings and pictures: they walk by faith in the King of kings.

Thank you, Lord, for imprinting me on the palm of your hand. Thank you for writing my name permanently in the Book of Life. These are the only tattoos I desire. And, Lord, thank you for being permanently imprinted on my heart. I love you. Amen.

Chapter 2

It's All Their Fault!

*U*nless you are totally dedicated to Advance Failure and Losing, you probably want to be a happy person. And happiness or unhappiness depends upon what you tell yourself. You're always telling yourself something. Take a moment and listen to your own thoughts. Do you ever say to yourself:

It's not my fault that I argue all the time. They're the ones who start all the fights.

The reason I'm overweight is because my mother is overweight. It's her fault.

Why should I apologize? I'm not the one who is wrong.

It's not my fault I'm late. Nobody reminded me what time it was getting to be.

Most of us blame somebody else for our problems, or point our

You will know the truth, and the truth will set you free.

John 8:32

17

finger at the other guy when things go wrong. Some people blame their troubles on their parents or teachers or friends or their church. What we tell *ourselves* is one of the biggest influences in our lives. It's not so important what goes on around you as what you tell yourself about it.

For instance, if it's raining outside you can tell yourself, "Hey, it's raining. Rain is a good thing." Or you can say, "Rain stinks." Whether it's raining or not is usually unimportant, but what you *tell* yourself about it *is*. If you tell yourself rain stinks, you'll believe it and you'll be unhappy about rainy weather.

Now here's a secret: You can tell yourself the truth. Or you can tell yourself what isn't true, thereby becoming a victim of what I call *misbelief*. A misbelief is believing something that's *not true*.

A misbelief to deal with today is, *It's awful if something is my fault.*

Think about it carefully. Why do you put the blame on other people all the time? You want other people to be wrong or at fault because, somewhere in your mind, you're thinking, *I hate to be wrong. I hate to be the one at fault. It's awful if something is my fault.*

When we do something wrong, we react in different ways. We may lie about it. Deny it and pretend we didn't do it. Blame somebody else. Feel guilty and stupid. Get mad at the world. Go to bed and try to forget the whole thing. Overeat. Take drugs. Smoke.

You tell yourself the truth by being open with yourself and the Lord Jesus. Tell yourself, "Come on, self, it's not so awful to be wrong or at fault. I'm a Christian and I can handle it. Being wrong doesn't mean I'm weak. Being at fault doesn't mean I'm dumb. I don't have to hurt myself over it."

Just because we make a mistake doesn't mean instant punishment. The world won't cave in. We can face mistakes, admit them and carry on.

The Word of God is your source of truth. Knowing

what God really thinks about you will set you free. "You will know the truth, and the truth will set you free" (John 8:32).

TODAY

Decide to stop defending yourself if you're responsible when something goes wrong. Tell yourself, "I'm not a bad person if something is my fault. The *truth* is, I don't have to be hard on myself. I don't have to punish myself. I am precious to God. I am a person of value."

Thank you, Lord, for showing me it's OK to be wrong, to be at fault. Thank you for helping me to drop my defenses and for being able to know the truth that sets me free. I choose NOW to drop the misbelief that it is awful to be at fault. Amen.

Chapter 3

The Person You Listen the Most to Is *You!*

A *misbelief* is something you tell yourself that simply is not true. It's not true, but you believe it is. That's why it is a misbelief.

All day long, you are constantly telling yourself things that are true or false—did you know that? You talk to you more than anyone else in the whole world. Your words and thoughts are constantly communicating ideas and beliefs to yourself.

In fact, everything in your life is a result of what you *think*. So it's important to discover what's going on in your thoughts. You may not realize that you're just filled with negative and gloomy misbelief, and that the things you tell yourself aren't true at all!

For it is with your heart that you believe and are justified, and it is with your mouth that you confess and are saved.
Romans 10:10

Here's the strategy for getting rid of misbeliefs in your life.

With the power of the Lord

Jesus Christ at work in your life, you can begin to sort out what you tell yourself. The Holy Spirit guides you into all truth and He will show you the thoughts that are true and not true.

First, look at the way you're behaving. Examine your feelings. If you are feeling guilty, angry, defensive and mean, chances are you have a misbelief somewhere in your mind. It's important to discover misbeliefs and get rid of them so you can get on with your exciting life as a child of the living God. He has a lot for you to do and see and learn. Through you, He can make a tremendous impact on your world, and you don't have time to sit around hung up on a lot of misbeliefs.

Second, replace the misbelief with the truth. Here's an example. Let's say you're dozing off in English class when the teacher drops a question on you, a dead giveaway like, "Who are the two main characters in *Romeo and Juliet?*" Your drooping eyelids flutter open as you hear yourself answer impetuously, "William Shakespeare and Ben Johnson."

You're horrified when you realize your mistake. You want to explain, but it's too late. The sound of laughter sticks with you all the way through the bus ride home. You could probably think a lot of bad things about yourself. But you can replace them with the truth. Take a look.

The misbelief (or lie)	The truth
It's awful to make a mistake.	I made a mistake and that's OK.
It's terrible to do something dumb.	I did something dumb, and I can admit it and
I *am* dumb.	still be OK.

You can also tell when you're harboring those misbeliefs by how vigorously you defend yourself. When you bare acting defensively, it's usually because you don't

think you have the right to make a mistake. You're being hard on *yourself*. *(Who did* write Romeo and Juliet anyhow?)

TODAY

Tell yourself, "When God created this world, He created it with a place and a plan for me. I'm not an outsider to the human race."

What you do with your life and your world is totally up to you. If you believe you can't make a mistake, or that it's awful to do something dumb, you will limit yourself and be afraid to try new things. You'll be nervous, fearful—instead of being open, enthusiastic and eager to discover new things. Jesus Christ is the Lord of your life. He has overcome the world and, because He has, so can you. Take your rightful place as a child of God now.

Thank you, Lord Jesus, for delivering me from misbeliefs that defeat and hurt me. Thank you for not limiting my potential. Thank you for giving me your Spirit of truth to guide me and live in me. Amen.

Chapter 4

Nervousness Can Be Good for You

You'd have thought it was a social and historical miracle. Bob actually asked Janet out on a date. He was picking her up at her house at six-thirty and they were going to a contemporary Christian music concert. Janet was a nervous wreck all that day.

She woke up early because she couldn't sleep. Before breakfast, she ate the ice cream she found in the freezer, and then had two bowls of cornflakes and a banana an hour later. As the morning wore on, she started a few fights with her younger brother—just three or four—yelled when she thought her sister took too long in the bathroom, and polished her fingernails twice. Before lunch, she took a shower and a bath—and removed the fingernail polish. She ate lunch (three

Never will I leave you; never will I forsake you.
Hebrews 13:5

24

tacos and a burrito) while watching cartoons on television and spent the rest of the day putting her hair in hot rollers, munching on sunflower seeds and listening to her Amy Grant records. Somewhere in between, she managed to clean her room and write "Bob and Jan" several hundred times on the back page of her English notebook.

When 6 o'clock rolled around, Janet was redressing for the fifteenth time. ("The blue sweater? No. The green one. No. Try the beige jacket with the cream colored shirt. No. Yes. No.") There just wasn't enough time. She'd never be ready when Bob arrived.

Bob showed up on time and chatted happily with Janet's parents in the living room while she frantically changed her shoes for the sixth time.

Somehow she survived the evening. (And so did Bob.) The next day her girlfriends at church wanted to know all about the evening. She had gained three pounds worrying about the date, but now she was Miss Cool.

"Were you nervous?" one of them asked.

Janet sighed casually, "Are you kidding? Why would I be nervous?" "Did you have fun?" someone else asked. "Fun? Oh, it was all right." It occurred to Janet— vaguely—that she'd been so preoccupied with her hair all evening she hadn't thought about fun.

"Well? Do you *like* him?"

"I don't know—" Janet answered, trying unsuccessfully to yawn. The girls squealed, "She was a nervous wreck! She's in *love*." Which only goes to prove that *not* being nervous at crucial times is *totally* abnormal and weird.

Jesus tells you to trust Him and not to let your heart be troubled. And the way you get to that point is to go through some nerve-wracking experiences. Then you realize in amazement, "Hey, I can get through this thing without falling apart in twelve million pieces."

TODAY

Mellow out.

*T*hank you, Lord Jesus, that I can overcome nervousness. Thank you for showing me that it's OK to feel nervous and that I'm not weird for these feelings. Thank you for loving me and never leaving me. Thank you for your peace. Amen.

Chapter 5

Who Me, N-n-n-nervous?

Do you call yourself a nervous person? Stop right now. In fact, today is a perfect day to stop calling yourself *all* negative names. Do you call yourself dumb? Fat? Ugly? Do you call yourself clumsy?

Be assured the Lord Jesus *never* calls you any of these things. He sees you as beautiful and terrific.

If you have feelings of nervousness, that's a different story. I never took an exam without feeling a little nervous. And meeting new people, going new places, auditioning, giving recitals or speeches, performing on stage— any of these experiences are bound to be laced with some nervousness. After all, we are all feeling people. The difference is that you don't have to be a victim,

Let the peace of heart which comes from Christ be always present in your hearts and lives, for this is your responsibility and privilege as members of his body. And always be thankful.

Colossians 3:15, TLB

27

allowing those negative feelings to wipe you out.

Two basic causes of nervousness are: You're afraid of what people will think of you; and you're afraid of failing and making a jerk of yourself. But the only difference between a failure and a success is that the successful person has failed more often.

Here's a little *Nervousness Emergency First Aid Kit* to carry around with you at all times:

- Tell yourself it's OK to feel nervous. You are perfectly normal. You're not weird, crazy, deranged or having a mental breakdown. You're just nervous.
- Tell yourself you won't run away from the situation. Your life belongs to Jesus Christ who helps you convert nervous energy into creative energy. (That sure beats starting to sweat and complain and worry.)
- Tell yourself people won't stone you if you fail. Nobody is going to hate you. God won't hate you. You won't hate you.
- Tell yourself immediately it's OK if I'm not Ms. or Mr. Popular. I give others the right *not* to like me. (That's a toughie, but try it. You'll be shocked at how sane you'll become.)

TODAY

When nervousness hits, take a deep breath and say, "I'm feeling nervous, that's all—just nervous. I *will* recover."

Dear Jesus, help me remember that you are with me at all times. You never leave me. I can be nervous and it won't kill me. I don't need to be afraid that people won't like me, or that I'll fail and make a jerk out of myself. You never think I'm a jerk. You love me. I love you, too, Lord. Thanks.

Chapter 6

Did You Really Say That?

Do you ever wish you hadn't said a certain thing?

Sometimes you can feel like you've put both feet into your mouth at the same time. You lose sleep worrying about what you've said. You're irritable and nervous over it. You're absolutely positive you made a fool of yourself. You're afraid of the consequences, or wonder if you were misunderstood.

You lament, "Oh, *why* did I say that? How do I get out of this one?"

How *do* you take back words you've spoken? Someone once said that our words are like tiny pillow feathers shaken into the wind. Flying in every direction by the thousand, it's impossible to gather them all up again no matter how frantically you try. They're

For out of the . . . heart the mouth speaks.
Matthew 12:34

29

blown into the wind and gone forever. Your words are like that. Once they've been spoken, you can't get them back.

Before you became a Christian, you might have been the kind of person who blurted out any old thing you felt like saying. But you can't always say exactly what you want to say. If you did, you'd be an out-of-control, raving person—or a babbling, complaining argumentative person. But the Holy Spirit wants to make each of us a brand-new person. The Lord Jesus wants to be Lord of your words. He wants to help you control your mouth.

But here you are, a *Christian*, and you've said something you wish you hadn't. There are two things to do immediately.

First, recognize the difference between a sin and a

blunder. A blunder is when you have embarrassed your-self—like Carol, who told a girlfriend she had a fierce crush on a guy she hardly knew in her sophomore French class, only to discover that her girlfriend was *his* girl-friend.

It would be sin, on the other hand, if Carol maliciously put down the guy in French class, calling him an airhead. (*That's* unkind and unchristian.)

Second, after you've identified sin or a blunder, tell the Lord all about it. Ask His forgiveness. (Don't leave out a single detail.) "Oh, Lord, you just wouldn't believe what I did—." (Yes, He would!) "Lord, I said, _____

_____

(fill in the blank). Please forgive me and help me act ra-tionally."

TODAY

Pray for wisdom in your words, and pray that the Holy Spirit will guard your mouth. The Bible says He will forgive your sins. You can be assured He will help you overcome the uncom-fortable habit of putting your foot in your mouth.

Lord, in the Psalms David prayed, "Let me not be ashamed." I'm asking you not to let me be ashamed ei-ther. I want to make things right and I want to touch this world with good, not harm. Be Lord of my words. Amen.

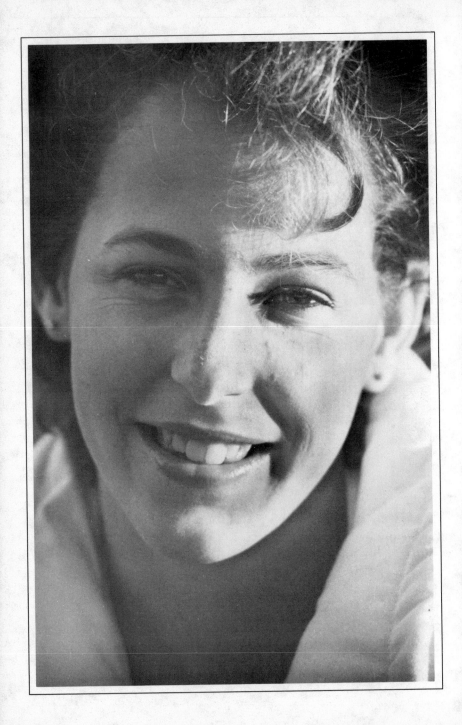

Chapter 7

If You Were Somebody Else, You'd Be Better Off, Right?

I always hated entering a new school. I had been to eight schools by the time I reached the ninth grade. I wished with all my heart that we could live in one house and I could go to one school so I didn't have to worry about making new friends all the time.

Once, in desperation, I introduced myself at a new school as Marcella D'Fabreaux from Paris. " 'allo, my name eez Marcella," I announced to the wide-eyed wonder of the other seventh graders. I was real popular—for a couple days. There in East Grand Forks, Minnesota, there weren't too many kids from "Paree" happening along.

"Say something in French." "What's it like in Paris?" "Do you have hamburgers over there?"

"*Oui, Oui*," I answered. That

For in Christ all the fullness of the Deity lives in bodily form, and you have been given fullness in Christ, who is the head over every power and authority.

Colossians 2:9, 10

33

was all the French I knew in this world besides "*Je m'ap-pelle Marcella*" and "*Où est la plume?*"

My ploy was discovered by a math teacher from Brus-sels who observed there wasn't a thing European about me. I had no choice then but to be old me again. What a bummer. Nobody cared if I lived or died as Marie. I could have come to school with a bowling ball for a head and nobody would have cared. But as Marcella I'd been a ce-lebrity!

Do you hear any misbeliefs here? For starters, there's: *I'm not good enough as I am.* I didn't feel good enough as a new seventh grader in East Grand Forks, Minnesota. So I made up a new person I thought would be more likeable.

I'm not good enough is a misbelief because it doesn't match up with the Word of God. David, who wrote many of the Psalms in the Bible, said, "I praise you because I am fearfully and wonderfully made; your works are won-derful, I know that full well" (Ps. 139:14). You, too, are fearfully and wonderfully made by God.

Because you are God's creation, you are a wonderful individual. You don't have to be somebody else. It's cru-cial to be able to see ourselves as God sees us. When God created you He saw you as a fun, happy, productive, full-of-ideas person. He saw you as creative, loveable and lov-ing. He didn't see you as self-conscious, defeated, grouchy and wiped out. Can you imagine God telling the angels, "I think I'll create a real nerd—a hopeless loser. Then I'll just sit back and watch him make a mess out of life." God isn't like that.

David was excited about the way God made him. He praised the Lord, "For you created my inmost being. . . . My frame was not hidden from you. . . . How precious to me are your thoughts, O God! How vast is the sum of them!" (Ps. 139:13, 15, 17).

As a seventh grader I was self-conscious and I wanted to be liked. It wasn't easy making new friends every time we moved. I wanted to fit in, to be special. Then the loving hand of God found me, and I discovered His acceptance. That's what has changed my life. And that's what will change yours.

Tell yourself you enjoy being you. Tell yourself you are going to enjoy the Lord Jesus. Today, you will begin to praise Him for making you exactly who you are, the way you are, and where you are.

The Misbelief	*The Truth*
I'm not OK.	I *am* OK. I'm fearfully and wonderfully made by God. I belong to Him. I reflect Him. I live in His love and I have His full attention. No place could be better than where I am right now.

TODAY

Remember that God doesn't create
losers.

*T*hank you, Lord Jesus, that in spite of my feelings and fears I am fearfully and wonderfully made. Nobody could be a better me than me. Amen.

Chapter 8

What You Give Away May Not Be Yours to Give

There's an old saying, "Only what you give away is really yours." We aren't limited to giving material gifts. We can give what seems impossible.

Two of Jesus' disciples, Peter and John, were at the temple for prayer one afternoon when a crippled beggar called to them, asking for money. They looked him straight in the eye and Peter said, "Silver and gold I do not have, but what I have I give you. In the name of Jesus Christ of Nazareth, walk" (Acts 3:6).

The crippled man had settled for coins until Peter and John challenged him with the impossible. The moment they helped him to his feet, the man's feet and ankles became strong. He was so excited he leaped and walked into the temple praising God.

The Sovereign Lord has given me an instructed tongue, to know the word that sustains the weary. He wakens me morning by morning, wakens my ear to listen like one being taught.

Isaiah 50:4

Peter and John saw beyond the crippled man's limitations. They were more aware of God's power than twisted, frail limbs. They had no money, no presents, no silver or gold, but they had faith and the power of the Holy Spirit in their lives. They knew the best gift they could give was the touch of God.

You may know some people who are struggling and hurting, who can't see any way out of their problems. It's as though they're crippled in their minds and hearts. They can't seem to walk. It's important to know what you cannot give them—and what you *can*.

Let's say you're talking with a person who has some heavy-duty problems. You can see beyond the impossible and you want to help.

Let's look first at what you *can't* do. There are some things you shouldn't expect of yourself. Don't try to come up with all the answers because you think that's what's expected of you. You'll be frustrated.

You can't possibly have all the answers because you aren't the guru of the universe. Jesus said, "Come to me, all you who are weary and burdened, and I will give you rest" (Matt. 11:28). It's safest to allow Jesus to be Savior and not try it yourself.

I know a sixteen-year-old girl who was complaining about her home life, and another sixteen-year-old counseled her to run away from home. The girl took her advice and the results were devastating. She nearly lost her life.

When somebody asks, "What should I do?" it's OK to say, "I don't know." You can be sympathetic and understanding. You might feel it's expected of you, but it's OK not to come up with solutions to somebody else's problems.

Two priceless gifts you can give are a listening ear and a compassionate heart. Silver and gold can't compare with them. If you can see beyond the impossible like Peter and John, you can give somebody encouragement and hope.

You can give your attention and demonstrate the love of God. You can pray with someone who is hurting. You'll bring His touch of love to places nobody else has.

TODAY

Realize you don't have all the answers.
But you can know and hear like the
One who does.

Lord Jesus, you told us to come to you because you know exactly what to do with heavy burdens and troubles. Give me the wisdom to know the words that help and the words that don't. Every day when I wake up, speak to me and teach me so that I reflect you and your loving and compassionate personality. Amen.

Chapter 9

Who Said Winners Never Quit?

If there ever was a winner, it was Moses.

The Bible says Moses was a friend of God. You don't get any higher than that. But even Moses had his off days.

In Numbers 20:8 God told Moses to gather the people together and, right *before their eyes*, speak to a rock so He could perform a miracle: The rock would gush out water enough for every man, woman and child and all the animals to drink. God knew the people were thirsty and complaining. Everything out there on the desert looked bleak, but God in His creative way had a plan.

So Moses started to do exactly as God commanded. He called all the people together in front of the rock. And then he blew it. Big. There he was, on the edge of a

Now if you obey me fully and keep my covenant, then out of all nations you will be my treasured possession. Although the whole earth is mine, you will be for me a kingdom of priests and a holy nation.

Exodus 19:5, 6

miracle and what did he do? He yelled at the people and called them a bunch of rebels. He got loud and angry and threw a little temper tantrum right there in front of all Israel and God. Then he swung his stick and whacked the rock. God was stunned. He told Moses in a way only God can, "You should have trusted me."

Yet God performed a miracle in spite of Moses' outburst and disobedience. Water gushed out from the rock, and the people and animals drank to their hearts' content.

It was a sad moment, though, because God wanted Moses to demonstrate something special by *speaking* to the rock. He wanted a holy spectacle, proof that He was a merciful, miracle-working God. And Moses blew it.

Still, the Bible says he was a friend of God. Even though Moses disobeyed God, God didn't throw him to the dogs and turn His back on him. You might say Moses was a man completely committed to God even though he made mistakes. Because he was committed, because he got up and kept going, he was a winner.

Even if you blow it, you're not a loser. You're a winner. Even though you might quit once in a while, you always come back. Winners never keep on hitting the rock. Winners learn what went wrong and pick up and start again. Just like Moses did.

TODAY

Think of yourself as a friend of God.
You're a person who refuses to keep
on failing to do God's perfect will, but
one who will get up and get going!

Dear Lord Jesus, thank you for giving me as many opportunities as I need to start over again. Thanks for not creating losers. Amen.

Chapter 10

Does Commitment Mean I'm Stuck?

Connie was on the cross-country team at her high school. One day she hobbled in to the locker room to shower after training, muttering, "I'm sick of coming in last. I've got blisters on top of blisters. My whole body is one big sore. I'm *quitting*."

Later, she faced the coach with her little speech about quitting the team. He was quiet and then said, "You can't quit, Connie. We're counting on you."

"But I can't do it. I'll never place. I'll always be in pain. No way."

"You *can't* quit," the coach repeated, "because you committed yourself to the team. Even if you don't run, you have to show up at the meets. You're *committed*."

Connie groaned. "What if I break my foot or get shin splints?"

Know therefore that the Lord your God is God; he is the faithful God, keeping his covenant of love to a thousand generations of those who love him and keep his commands.

Deuteronomy 7:9

41

"You'll still be on the team. You'll have to sit out the meets at the sidelines."

Connie went home feeling angry and helpless.

The next week, Connie told her coach, "I didn't know commitment meant not being able to quit! I don't think I've ever been truly committed to anything in my whole life." This was serious. She was beginning to see, for the first time, that feelings don't dictate commitment.

Can you say today you're truly committed to God? Do you feel like a quitter at times? If you do, tell yourself, *All winners have to face the desire to quit. They have to decide whether or not to go with the feelings.*

Commitment means you cannot quit. You cannot quit, no matter what your feelings are. Moses blew it at Kadesh by hitting the rock instead of talking to it as God had commanded. But Moses was *still* God's friend.

TODAY

> Will you commit your life to Jesus Christ totally? Will you accept yourself as a person who is precious to Him? Will you see yourself as beautifully stuck to Him forever as His friend?

Dear Lord Jesus you are faithful. You said you will keep your promises to your children for a thousand generations. I give myself totally to you now, I commit my life to you and realize once and for all our relationship is a forever one. Even if I blow it, you don't give up on me. You were committed to me enough to die on the cross so I could be forgiven and made clean. Ours is an eternal relationship. Amen.

Chapter 11

Stuffing Your Feelings

Did you know anger is not always a sin? The simple *brief* emotion of anger is normal. The Bible gives two views of anger. Ephesians 4:26 says; "In your anger do not sin: Do not let the sun go down while you are still angry," and in James 1:19 it reads; "Everyone should be quick to listen, slow to speak and slow to become angry, for man's anger does not bring about the righteous life that God desires."

Temper tantrums, rage, throwing things or shouting cruel words is not exactly the greatest behavior. You can probably think of better ways to spend your time, right? On the other hand, how about those angry feelings you don't express openly? Maybe you "stuff" angry feelings. There you are, smiling outwardly—but with

Refrain from anger and turn from wrath; do not fret—it leads only to evil.
Psalm 37:8

clenched teeth because inwardly you're seething.

Acting out anger and stuffing anger are both inappropriate ways of dealing with your emotions. Long-term "stuffing" can turn you into a bitter, resentful person, and uncontrolled temper tantrums are just plain poisonous.

Jesus wants to help you understand your emotions and express them in the right way. He wants you to live happily with them. He is making you a new person from the inside out.

TODAY

Tell yourself anger in itself is not bad. Admit it when you feel angry. "I feel angry because my feelings were hurt," or "I was mistreated," or "I lost something." You fill in the reason. Then admit your feelings to the Lord. *Don't wait*. Once you've aired your feelings to Him, ask Him to give you wisdom and understanding in how to handle the problem that made you angry. He will.

*F*ather, in the name of Jesus, help me to accept and understand my emotions in light of your Word. Today I choose to face my angry feelings, to stop "stuffing" them and also to end temper tantrums. Amen.

Chapter 12

The Famous Little White Lie

Jerry likes to "beef up" the number of points he scores alone in basketball practice.

Carol steps outside on the front porch when the phone rings when it's someone she doesn't want to talk to. That way her sister can say Carol is "out."

Phyllis is late for every youth meeting. She always hopes there'll be a car stopped along the freeway, so she can claim that traffic was "backed up for miles."

Bill slips the change from his dad's $20 bill in his dresser drawer and insists it took every cent to put gas in the car.

Is there any such thing as a "little white lie"? Calling it that soothes your conscience—or does it?

These lies can seem harmless but actually they're not harmless

My Child, if your heart is wise, my heart will be glad. . . . Yes, my heart will rejoice when your lips speak right things.

Proverbs 23:15,
Amplified

at all. They're quite dangerous. They make wrong look acceptable. But Proverbs 10:5 says: *"He that speaks lies shall not escape."*

Hold it, you say. Everybody lies about being late. Everybody steals. Everybody cheats. The truth is, people who do those things get into trouble. If you want to be one of them, you are opening yourself up to defeat.

You see, once you get used to lying about "little" things, the devil can influence you to lie about something big. It starts with a lie that seems harmless. You might even think it's the best thing to do in a certain situation.

Every time we cover for ourselves in this way, it's because we've told ourselves a lie. We have accepted the misbelief that lying is sometimes OK—that it's acceptable, and not really a violation of God's law.

Can you find anywhere in the Bible where telling a little white lie is OK?

- Abraham told a little white lie, you might say, when he called his wife his sister.
- Peter might have thought it was just a little white lie when he said he didn't know Jesus.
- Potiphar's wife might have even convinced herself that it was just a little white lie when she falsely accused Joseph of breaking into her room and assaulting her.
- And while we're looking at lies, do you think Adam and Eve might have convinced themselves it was only a little white lie when they told God they hadn't done anything wrong?

All of these lies had consequences. All were evil in God's sight.

TODAY

Ask the Lord to help you know the truth about the little white lie. No lie is white, and no lie is little. Lying is making yourself the judge of what's right and wrong. That's God's position. He wants you to take Him at His word, and trust Him to help you be unashamed and unafraid of the truth.

I choose today, Lord Jesus, to be a person who speaks the truth. Show me when I lie, Lord. Show me those little white lies that you hate. I want to please you and not run away from facing truth. Amen.

Chapter 13

Saying No To Yourself

I hate that word *self-control*," Renee fumed. "Every time I turn around I have to give up something."

What does self-control mean to you? Does it mean dieting, going without, sacrifice, pain, gritting your teeth and forcing yourself to do something you hate? Is it agony and sheer misery?

One girl told me self-control meant going on a diet to lose weight. Another told me self-control meant she had to practice the piano every single day no matter what. A couple of guys told me self-control meant being on time and not getting angry. Another told me he had self-control when he kept his mouth shut and kept his cool when his little sister tried to pick a fight with him. Another

If anyone would come after me, he must deny himself and take up his cross and follow me.

Matthew 16:24

told me it was saying no to drugs.

Do you hate the words self-control? If you do, here's an encouraging thought for you. Did you know you already are exercising self-control in many ways? Chances are, you don't give yourself much credit for the self-control you show every single day. When was the last time you told yourself "Good for me" when you brushed your teeth, or when you didn't go back to sleep after the alarm went off? Have you ever given yourself a pat on the back for not smoking when a lot of the other kids at school smoke? You may say, "Those things are *easy*. What's the big deal?"

I say, "Why do you think self-control has to be *hard*?"

You probably have more self-control than you think. But you probably are not in the habit of rewarding yourself. Most people think they should only be rewarded for *pain*. How about rewarding yourself for doing something that's easy? After all, everything you do is out of choice.

Besides, denying yourself doesn't have to be all that painful. Some people think of self-control in the same category as death and dismemberment. It's just the pits. The very thought of it is like life imprisonment for a crime never committed.

How do you define self-control? Is it really all that hard for you to deny yourself something you want badly? Or to resist something you know is bad for you? How do you feel when you're forced to endure discomfort, interruption, delay or mixed up plans? Is it truly the absolute worst?

It's not always easy to deny yourself, to go without something you want, or to give up something you like. But sometimes, for the sake of a better, happier you and a deeper walk with God, it's necessary. Most of the time, in fact, you'll find that gaining something incredibly wonderful in your life actually depends on how much discomfort and frustration you can take.

Have you ever noticed that your greatest and most dazzling achievements have been won because you were willing to put up with pain or something downright *unpleasant*?

You *can* deny yourself. You *can* say no to yourself. It's not the end of the world if you have to suffer. You can stand it. Really you can. It's not *always* difficult and painful.

TODAY

Remember, not all self-control is painful. It can be fun and challenging if you make it that way.

Thank you, Lord, for giving me the fruit of self-control. Thank you for helping me overcome temptation and deny myself. Thank you for showing me that I can do it. I can say no! And it doesn't always have to be painful! Amen.

Chapter 14

Self-Control Is Not a Dirty Word

*R*enee, who hates self-control, you will recall, needed to lose twenty pounds.

"But I *like* food," she complained. "I *hate* cottage cheese and lettuce. I wish I had been born skinny with an inborn hatred for fattening food." Renee was sure she came into this world with a hamburger in one hand and a chocolate shake in the other. She was "born chubby" and stayed that way.

She began her diet to lose twenty pounds—and became an instant monster. Renee was so disagreeable her friends begged her to throw away the cottage cheese and lettuce and eat a candy bar instead. She was like a small child who was being denied some treat or toy. Eventually, she was able to bring her eating under

> No temptation has seized you except what is common to man. And God is faithful; he will not let you be tempted beyond what you can bear. But when you are tempted, he will also provide a way out so that you can stand up under it.
>
> *1 Corinthians 10:13*

control and she lost weight. She was a happier person when she could say no to herself and not expire on the spot.

Renee learned that saying no to dessert was not the same as being sent away from the table for being a bad girl. She discovered that denying herself sweets gave her a better self-image via a slimmer body. She learned to tell herself the truth: "It's good to say no to my appetite. It's good to have self-control. It's creative and fun. It's a privilege."

TODAY

Tell yourself the truth.

*F*ather, *in the name of Jesus, I will take up my cross and follow my Savior and Lord. I will love Him with all my heart, soul and mind, and I will discover the joy in self-denial and self-control. Amen.*

Chapter 15

The Guy Who Has It All Together Could Be Falling Apart

*F*red was known as the class nerd. He was always on the outside of what was happening. He just never seemed to be quite "with it." If everybody wore jeans, he wore dress slacks. If everybody rode a skateboard, he rode a Moped. He carried his lunch in a Star Wars lunch box. And during a school assembly, he would rise to his feet after the announcements to give the principal a standing ovation.

Then there was Ted. He was the coolest, wildest, most stylish guy in the entire school. He was the guy every other guy tried to emulate. Girls adored him. He was a trend-setter, an innovator. Nobody messed around with Ted. He was boss.

Fred and Ted were in the same class but they were worlds apart.

So then, each of us will give an account of himself to God.

Romans 14:12

After graduation the most incredible thing happened. Fred won a scholarship to an Ivy League college in the east and Ted went on to charm the partying gang in his neighborhood while working parttime at a local gas station. A few years later, Fred was in graduate school getting a master's degree in education and Ted was becoming an alcoholic.

At a class reunion ten years later, Fred was the only Ph.D. there. Ted was unable to attend the event as he was in treatment in a drug and alcohol rehabilitation center where he had been since his third arrest and conviction for driving under the influence.

Sometimes we look on the outside of things before we check out what's going on underneath. What drives a person to be popular? Why do you dislike nerds? Why is it so important to look like you've got it all together even if you don't?

Here's a common misbelief: *What I am on the outside is far more important than what I am or feel on the inside.* And here's another one: *What people think of me is the most important thing in life.*

If you believe those two lies, you might hide your Barbie dolls or put your electric train in the garage so nobody knows you've got them, but what about when you do everything "right" and you *still* don't get the acceptance of the "cool" crowd?

Fred didn't care whether he was accepted or not. He didn't seem to mind being the class nerd. He did his own thing and was satisfied with the few good friends he had. Ted, on the other hand, with his natural good looks was driven to succeed, to earn popularity and acceptance. He worked hard at being charming and cool. He couldn't tolerate rejection. Ultimately he rejected himself by choosing self destructive behaviors such as his drinking.

TODY

Tell yourself, "God sees me from the
inside. He hears my thoughts and
knows my dreams and goals. He cares
about my needs for acceptance. He
loves me and never rejects me."

*Lord Jesus, today I will live to please you, not others.
Today I choose to appreciate you and accept your love.
Amen.*

Chapter 16

What Makes You Feel Angry?

Cheryl and Lee Ann walked together to the bus stop after school. "It's not fair," Cheryl complained angrily. "My parents let my brother drive when *he* was sixteen. They make *me* wait another year." Cheryl became angrier as they walked. "My parents *always* let my brother do things I can't do. They treat me like a *baby*."

Lee Ann was quiet. She didn't have her driver's license yet either. As they reached the corner, Cheryl continued to steam. "They treat me like I'm totally irresponsible. I *hate* the way they think I'm just a little kid! I think I'll move out. Get my own apartment."

"Maybe you're being hotheaded," Lee Ann offered, delicately.

Cheryl exploded. "How can

A wise man fears the Lord and shuns evil, but a fool is hotheaded and reckless. A quick-tempered man does foolish things, and a crafty man is hated.
Proverbs 14:16, 17

you say that? I am *not* being hotheaded! *You're* just being judgmental!" Miserably she marched off in the opposite direction, leaving Lee Ann standing alone on the curb.

"Cheryl, you'll miss the bus!" Lee Ann called after her. Cheryl only walked faster, pounding her heels on the sidewalk with every step.

And yes, she did miss the bus.

Do you think Cheryl had good reason to snap at her friend? Do you see any misbeliefs in her dialogue?

We become angry because of what we believe, not because of what happens to us. Lee Ann was in the same situation as Cheryl. She wasn't allowed to drive yet, or to have her own car either. But Lee Ann wasn't warped out of shape over it. Why? Because of what she *told* herself about the situation.

Cheryl had some very definite misbeliefs:

- I should get what I want.
- Nobody should criticize me.
- Nobody else's feelings are as important as mine.

These are *misbeliefs* because they are beliefs that are off-center; they aren't God-centered. Cheryl didn't get what she wanted, so she became furious. She also believed nobody should ever criticize her, so she lashed out at Lee Ann, hurting her feelings. Cheryl didn't realize Lee Ann's feelings were important, too.

The Bible teaches us to be wise and reject evil. Misbeliefs can be evil because they keep us from living happy, full lives in Christ. They keep us from being a blessing to anybody else, too.

Cheryl had to call Lee Ann later that night to apologize. She had been reading the Proverbs in her Bible and saw the words, ". . . a quick-tempered man does foolish things." It hit right where it hurt. On the phone she said, "You're right, Lee Ann, I was being hotheaded. I'm sorry." She had missed the bus and had to walk six miles home carrying a heavy armload of books and wearing shoes that gave her blisters.

After she calmed down, Cheryl recognized her misbeliefs and was able to pray and replace them with the truth. She surrendered her thoughts and feelings to the Lord Jesus and asked Him to forgive her. Then she told her parents calmly, "I really want to drive a car now that I'm sixteen. But it's not the end of the world if I don't. I hope we can discuss it again soon, especially since I'll be taking Driver's Ed next semester if it's OK with you."

Cheryl's temper is by no means a thing of the past yet. She has to work at it. She admits that she has a ways to go before she will be able to feel free and released from her negative thinking habits. But she's getting there.

TODAY

Allow the presence of the Holy Spirit to permeate your entire being. Feel His peace and His level-headedness. Feel God in you. Then trust yourself and allow the smile in your heart to warm you all over.

Father, I know I do not have to get exactly what I want. I can allow things to go wrong without falling apart. I can handle interference in my plans and I can take criticism responsibly. I can do these things because I am totally yours and seeking your wisdom and will for my life. I will not accept hotheaded behavior as OK. I will accept your love and your wisdom. Amen.

Chapter 17

Can Plastic Surgery Help This Face?

The woman meant well when she said to Cindy, "With a face like yours, I'm sure you sing like an angel," but Cindy didn't catch the compliment.

"I hate this nose," she complained. "I hate this hair." And while she was at it, she added, "And I hate my voice."

When I was the star chubette at my dear old high school, I couldn't name a thing about myself I liked. My mother always told me, "Honey, you may not be Miss America, but you've got nice teeth." My aunt Kay told me once—and I'll never forget it until the day I die, because it was the nicest thing anybody ever said to me up till then—"Marie, you have expressive eyes." (To this day whenever anybody takes my picture, I roll my eyes and flash

Commit thy works unto the Lord, and thy thoughts shall be established.

Proverbs 16:3, KJV

my teeth. That's why I always look like Bozo the clown on my photographs, but I'm just trying to show off my good points.)

But let's get back to Cindy. She was in the youth group I was leading, and I must say she wasn't really what you'd call a dazzling beauty. She wore men's boots, combed her hair straight over her face (to hide her faint mustache), and slouched around as if she were carrying the weight of the entire universe on her two rather hefty shoulders. Cindy came to me all upset because she didn't think anybody liked her. She didn't think God did either. I wanted to suggest that God might like her a lot better if she stopped beating up the boys, but I resisted the urge.

"Cindy," I said, "I believe God created this world for you, so you could make something good of it. I believe it's up to you what you do with it."

One eye peered out from the strings of hair covering her face. "Huh?"

"You can go on telling yourself a lot of lies like, 'Nobody likes me and God doesn't either.' Or you can take the love God has for you and make it your *reality*."

She told me she felt ugly. I told her we all do at times. She told me she didn't have a dad. I told her neither did I. She told me she broke her nose in 1984. I told her that was the same year I was in a bicycle accident and broke my neck. We had a lot in common.

I wish I could tell you that because of our talks Cindy went on to become a raving beauty on the silver screen, but that's not quite what happened. She did make great strides with Jesus, however. And one day she told me, "I know one of my misbeliefs—want to hear it?" I was all ears. "It's this: *It's terrible not to be beautiful*—that's a misbelief!"

What a great realization. "And here's another one," she went on. *"If I'm not beautiful, I'm a terrible person."*

Then she told me she had replaced the misbeliefs with the truth. She grinned (and I noticed she no longer had the mustache). While she was talking I also noticed her hair was cut and combed. Here's what she said: "It's not true that it's terrible not to be beautiful. A person can learn to use what he's got and that's not bad. Looks have nothing to do with whether a person is good or bad. I am not a terrible person. Jesus loves me!"

I gave her a big hug. "Cindy, that's incredible. You're beautiful!"

We laughed together and before she left, she turned at the door and said, "I remembered what you said. God created the world for me so I could make something good out of it. I decided to do that."

TODAY

Look at yourself in the mirror and say,
"You are precious to the Lord Jesus!"

Thank you, Lord Jesus, for showing me how to change into a person I like. Thank you for taking away the lie that I can't help myself. Thank you for giving me the privilege of being able to make something good happen in my world. I commit my works unto you so that my thoughts are established where they ought to be—in you! Amen.

Chapter 18

Everybody Is Doing It—What About You?

*T*hey called her "Red" because of the tattoo on her arm: a dragon with blood dripping from its mouth.

Red was fifteen. Her hair stood up in a high-spiked, purple mohawk. She wore four earrings on each ear, a gold stud on one side of her nose and her eyes were painted with thick, black liner and sparkly gold shadow. She wore a black leather halter and skirt, fishnet hose and 60 bicycle chains around her stomach, neck and hips. On her feet were heavy boots with spiked heels and toes, and in her pockets she carried a pair of brass knuckles and enough cocaine to last her two days.

She was heading toward the supermarket to buy cigarettes when three Christian girls I know approached her in the parking lot

Blessed is the man who does not walk in the counsel of the wicked or stand in the way of sinners or sit in the seat of mockers.

Psalm 1:1

and started a conversation. Red was in a hurry and didn't want to stop, but she stayed and talked with the girls. Soon they were telling her about Jesus, King of kings and Savior. Before long, Red was in tears. She prayed with her new friends, asking Jesus to be Lord of her life.

Red told the girls later she had planned to beat somebody up and kill them that night.

Not long after, Red also changed her name back to her given name, Rebecca. She continued to learn more about Christ and commit every area of her life to Him. She changed radically. Her life was an undeniable example, and she was greatly loved in her church.

Rebecca was committed to God and nothing could intimidate her. She was fearless and outspoken. Some of her old Punk enemies threatened her life and she told one of them, "You come near me, baby, and the Lord will ZAP you! I'm not Red now. I'm not carrying drugs. I'm not a fighter. I'm committed to Jesus Christ and Him only."

She has led many of her old friends to the Lord. A year after she became a Christian, Rebecca was horrified to see that two of the same girls who led her to Christ were turning to the very things she had been saved from. She pounced on them.

"Where's your *commitment*?" she demanded. "Are you so dumb that you think Satan can offer you something better than God? I can't understand how a person can say he loves Jesus and not be committed to living for Him. I will never do drugs again. I'll never ever drink or smoke. Never. That's over. I'll never listen to destructive worldly music. I'll never go back to the same places. I am talking never. My life belongs to God. I remind myself of that every day.

"Anybody who thinks he can dabble in sin and still love Jesus is only kidding himself. Sooner or later the lifestyle gets you."

Rebecca tells other teenagers, "You're kidding yourselves if you think you can get messed up in worldly life and not pay a price. You jump in the fire, baby, and you get burned. You play with demons and you get wiped out."

Then she gives the good news: "But if you're committed to Jesus Christ and living for Him only, He saves you from eternal hell *and* hell on earth."

Sooner or later you're going to be confronted with temptation to "try" things you know you shouldn't. The excuse is always the same: "It looks like fun—and everybody else is doing it." But the devil doesn't play fair. His "toys" are really deadly weapons.

"Be self-controlled and alert. Your enemy the devil prowls around like a roaring lion looking for someone to devour" (1 Pet. 5:8).

TODAY

Remind yourself how precious you and your body are. Someone with such worth doesn't deserve the poisons of the devil.

Lord Jesus, keep your mind in me so I choose your blessings and not the devil's poison. I choose to bless myself with the good things you give and I choose to take your blessings and your joy as my way of life. Amen.

Chapter 19

Forming Good Habits

Maybe drugs, alcohol and sex haven't been a problem in your school. Maybe you're not tempted daily by demonic music, bizarre clothing, swearing and negative talk. Maybe you're just not the type to smoke, drink, or do drugs. But in spite of your safe position, you have to make a lifestyle commitment. If you don't you will slowly drift away from God.

Christians drift for two reasons: First, they aren't committed to Jesus Christ with their entire life, and second, they misbelieve there is something OK about sinning. Like the girl who says, "Going out with a guy who isn't a Christian may not be good, but it's better than not going out at all." No commitment; no common sense.

You can make a habit of re-

Submit yourselves, then, to God. Resist the devil, and he will flee from you.
James 4:7

sisting the devil. If you resist the devil today, and then you resist another temptation he throws at you tomorrow, and the day after, too, you'll be a lot better prepared to handle the temptations the next day and the next. Make a habit of turning away from temptation, and you will build an inner strength that will be a powerful source of help to you all your life.

Jesus said, "abide in me." In other words, hang in there. Form habits. Get addicted to *not* smoking; get hooked on *not* following the crowd when sin is "in."

Get in the habit of being totally dependent upon the Lord. Get in the habit of reading the Word every single day. Read this book as a help along with your Bible. Stop thinking of yourself as weak and needy. As a Christian you are strong and free because Jesus says you are.

TODAY

> Memorize John 15:5: "I am the vine; you are the branches. If a man remains in me and I in him, he will bear much fruit; apart from me you can do nothing."

In the mighty name of Jesus, I turn away the work of the devil and I resist his lies! I submit myself totally to the Lord Jesus and choose to bear fruit for You! Amen.

Chapter 20

Best Friends

My best friend's name in high-school was LaRee Hamlett. Her birthday was in July and mine was in October so that made her four months older than I and more mature. In spite of the age difference, we were absolute true-blue buddies. We swore faithful allegiance to each other for all eternity. Nothing on the face of this earth could separate us or in any way mar, disturb or interfere with our perfect friendship.

LaRee was the greatest best friend a girl could have, I thought. We worked out all sorts of differences. For instance, she was Catholic and I was Lutheran, so we took turns going to St. Lawrence and Hope Lutheran. We loved the Lord, but to be honest we were more interested in the boys than in the liturgy at church.

I have loved you with an everlasting love; I have drawn you with loving-kindness.
Jeremiah 31:3

70

Boys were God's greatest invention since department stores. And here's where our perfect friendship hit a snare. LaRee was more popular with boys than I was. Let me tell you, it was perilous.

LaRee was skinny, and she had dark hair, dark eyes and perfect skin. I was short, never thin (even though my mother insisted the fat was in my head), and my skin was never perfect. My hair was nondescript until I began dumping hydrogen peroxide over it, becoming an instant pumpkin-colored blonde.

I always felt inferior to LaRee, but I was enormously proud of her because she was my best friend. (I had my good teeth, after all. Hers were just so-so.) I was never jealous of LaRee—just sort of inferior feeling.

After we graduated from high school, I headed for New York to go to school and prepare for a career in the theater. LaRee followed soon after and we became roommates. One day she told me the most amazing thing. She said, "Marie, we've known each other most of our lives and there has hardly been a time when I haven't felt inferior to you. You're such an exciting person and I'm so dull."

I could have croaked on the spot.

She felt inferior? Next to her I felt like chopped liver. Which only proves you never know what a person is thinking. But even more than that, it shows you how comparison thinking can rob you of self-esteem. All through my growing-up years, I compared myself to other people. If LaRee was prettier, that meant I was ugly. If somebody else had a great voice, my voice automatically sounded like zilch.

In New York, LaRee entered nursing school and moved into the school dorm at the hospital. We continued to be proud of each other's pursuits and maintain our friendship, but after we were both married, we sort of lost touch. She went to graduate school, I had babies. Then I went on to college and graduate school, and our letters became less and less frequent. It never occurred to us, not in our wildest dreams, that we would never see each other again.

LaRee died alone in her New York apartment. She was dead for a week before her body was discovered. Somebody said, "She was so beautiful. She had everything."

There are so many things I wish I could have told her. Like I wish we could have talked just one more time about the one Best Friend who never leaves or forsakes us. I wish I could have heard her pray just one more time. I wish I could have told her how she taught me that I am forever an OK person because I was once someone's best friend. I wanted to tell her that I learned so late about inferiority being a sin, to ask her if she had learned that, too.

TODAY

Take a mental inventory. Whom do you compare yourself with? Make a vow to stop it. Comparison thinking will make mincemeat out of you.

Lord Jesus, thank you for loving us with an everlasting love. Thank you for constantly drawing us toward yourself. You don't ever want us to feel inferior. You want us to see ourselves as you see us.

Lord, will you be my friend?

Chapter 21

"With-It" Thinking

With-It thinking is reality. It's true according to God's Word. It's rational, sensible and logical in God's mind.

Not-With-It thinking is unreasonable. These thoughts *seem* true, but they aren't because they don't follow God's thoughts. God's reality is the way things are.

With-It thinking is productive, good, true. It's not pretending to be OK, it *is* OK. With-It thinking leads to achievement of goals, appropriate emotions, and feelings of worth and being an OK person.

Not-With-It thinking leads to self-defeat, gloom, not achieving goals and emotional confusion.

Look at the list that follows and place a check in the column that tells what each statement is

Do not let any unwholesome talk come out of your mouths, but only what is helpful for building others up according to their needs, that it may benefit those who listen.

Ephesians 4:29

to you. Be real. Remember, you're not some toad in the great swamp of life.

	True	Not True
Nobody in the world will ever be my friend.	____	____
I would be happier at school if I got straight A's in my classes.	____	____
I never do anything right.	____	____
I'm bad at sports and bad at school so I must be a bad person.	____	____
Everybody hates me.	____	____
I'd like to have more friends at school.	____	____
I hate all jocks.	____	____

Your score: If you checked three or more true, thinking you're making a With-It answer, you are a negative thinking person. Chances are you get depressed a lot and go from feeling great to being in the pits.

If you checked one true, you got a perfect score. The only With-It statement on the list was, "I'd like to have more friends at school." It's a rational thing to say. "I'll die if I don't make more friends" is not rational. Those kinds of thoughts will make you very unhappy and uptight.

We're learning how to watch for unwholesome talk coming out of our mouths. By unwholesome I mean *anything* that puts you down or hurts you. Each one of us directly affects at least fifteen people in our personal world. If your mind is loaded with ugly, untrue thoughts, you not only hurt yourself, you hurt at least fifteen others.

The Lord Jesus Christ, your Lord and Savior, is right there with you guiding you, reminding you and showing you just how dynamic and beautiful you can be in Him.

TODAY

Decide to be real in an unreal world.

*F*ather, I choose to be more aware of the words I speak every day. I will let no unwholesome talk come out of my mouth. I'm going to work at it and have fun doing it. Show me your reality and release to me a new understanding of your With-It thinking!

Chapter 22

Is an Aptitude for Algebra in the Genes?

When I was in high school we
had a school song that went like
this: "Wave the flag for dear old
Marshall, lift her banners high.
There's no school like dear old
Marshall, and here's the reason
why, rah-rah-rah . . ." We all
thought it was a dumb song but
"dear old" was sort of appropriate.

That school was *really* old.
My mother went to John Marshall
and I actually had some of the
teachers she'd had. My mother
had been a perfect straight-A student.

When I was about fifteen, I
wondered if there was a mistake
made at the hospital when I was
born. Obviously I'd been given to
the wrong family. I came up with
this theory when Mrs. Montank,
my World History teacher, kept
me after class one day.

*Whatever you do, work at
it with all your heart, as
working for the Lord, not
for men.*
Colossians 3:23

She glared at me over the top of her glasses and said, "Your mother never talked out of turn in class, Marie. Your mother always handed in assignments on time. Your mother never straggled into the room after the last bell. She came to class prepared and took her studies seriously. Are you sure you're your mother's daughter?"

My darkest suspicions loomed before me. So! I wasn't my mother's daughter! My *real* mother was probably a hilarious, high-spirited adventurer who had no interest in world history, who thought the Industrial Revolution was a bathroom cleanser. Right at that very moment she was probably eeking out a meager existence as a coffeehouse comic, or a street mime or circus clown, all because she hadn't taken 10th-grade World History seriously. She had joked and dreamed her way through high school like I was doing instead of being an honors student like my "present" mom.

I went home and told my mother—the one who got straight A's—that I was dropping out of school to search for my *real* mother, the one who barely made C+'s. "My real mother is not good at math," I lamented, "and I take after her. No sense in going on. I'm doomed to follow in her footsteps."

I didn't want to face the fact that doing well in school was a matter of choice. I wanted to believe that an interest in algebra was something you inherited along with the color of your eyes or hair. I seemed to be the only one in the family with a passion for drama and art, so I figured I couldn't possibly be one of them. The truth is, we don't inherit our abilities, we develop them. We don't inherit enthusiasm, we create it. We don't inherit talent, we work at it. We don't inherit interests, we discover them. And we don't inherit bad habits and behavior, we choose them.

A heavy-duty misbelief is, "*I'm not responsible for me or what I do.*"

The truth is, "*I'm the only one who decides to do what I do.*"

Everything you do in your life is preceded by your choosing to do it. You choose to study, or you choose not to. You choose to like one thing over another. You choose to disrupt a class or not to. You choose to be late or on time. You really are not a victim of circumstances. And you really don't inherit your personality. When somebody says, "Oh, you're just like your grandpa," or "You talk just like your mom," realize that it's because you *choose* to be like them.

You choose to obey God or not to. You choose to surrender your life to Him, or you choose to float around dumbly on the sea of life not knowing to whom you belong.

TODAY

Choose to make Jesus Christ your hero
and role model and be just like *Him*.

Thank you, Lord Jesus, for the gift of choice. Thank you for making me uniquely different and uniquely me. Thank you for making me responsible for my choices. Today I choose you in all I do and think. Amen.

Chapter 23

Tomatoes Aren't All That Heavy

*I*t took me only about a week to decide against trying to find my "real" mother and my "real" family. I figured Christmas was coming and that would be bad timing to be moving and switching families. But it took a while before I could look Mrs. Montank in the eye. I wanted to write on the top of each history paper: THIS PAPER IS NOT MY FAULT. I'M ADOPTED AND NOT MY REAL SELF.

Besides, nobody seemed to take me seriously. When I told my mother I was packing and leaving home, she said, "Not until you do the dishes, young lady." I felt totally misunderstood, an artist without a palette.

When I screamed, "I'm leaving this road stand to find my real self!" my little brother (of whom

The word is near you; it is in your mouth and in your heart, that is, the word of faith.

Romans 10:8

80

I expected better) said, "I hope you're not taking your bike!"

The last straw was when I fell on my knees before my father (as I had seen in the movies), begging him to let me leave home in search of my true identity. Instead of rising up like an elephant in alarm, he sighed and fell asleep in his chair. There I knelt, with no alternative but to accept things as they were. (More about dullness and boredom later.) I had to face—horrors!—*reality*.

Young people are always asking me, "Dr. Chapian, what is reality?" This question is usually asked as if "reality" is some deep, dark, sacred, hushed and holy concept. I usually answer in my most mystical voice, "Reality, my darling, is—a huge bag of tomatoes. You can eat them, study them, give them away, or you can throw them at people. One thing is for certain, you have to do *something* with them. You can't just ignore them, because they'll turn rotten."

That day, a thousand years ago, I felt as if I were holding a bag of tomatoes in my arms and had nowhere to put them. I wanted to complain, blame somebody else for my troubles.

But our reality is God's reality and He tells us, "I write to you, young [people], because you are strong, and the word of God lives in you, and you have overcome the evil one" (1 John 2:14).

Strong and overcoming! That's what we want to be, isn't it? These are the words that can live in our hearts. These are the words we can speak. It's important we tell ourselves the truth—and the truth is, we're far more clever and strong than we realize.

When you're burdened with reality like a bag of fat, ripe tomatoes, make spaghetti sauce!

TODAY

Give a tomato to a friend.

I accept where I'm at right now in my life. I can carry my own burdens and allow the power of God to show me how. I am an overcomer! I overcome the evil one and the lie that tells me I'm weak and that my problems are because of somebody else. I speak these words to you, Jesus, so you'll hear them and bless them and make them real. I love you! Amen.

Chapter 24

Stop Throwing Tomatoes at Yourself

*T*heatergoers in the early 1900s threw tomatoes at the stage if they didn't like the performance. There are still opera houses today in Europe where audiences will throw tomatoes at the performers to show their displeasure. That's bad enough, but how about the person who throws tomatoes at himself when things don't go right?

Is that what you're like? Do you throw tomatoes at yourself when you make a mistake, or when you aren't perfect?

Sounds dumb, doesn't it? Can you imagine walking into a rest room and seeing some guy throwing tomatoes at his face in the mirror?

You might not actually keep a stash of tomatoes by your mirror, but you might as well. You throw

How great is the love the Father has lavished on us, that we should be called children of God!
John 3:1

tomatoes at yourself in a lot of different ways. You do it when you

Lie
Hide
Pretend
Quit

Lying says you're not OK where you're at right now. If you tell lies about anything at all, you are the one who is deceived. You're deceived because you must believe that someone will disapprove of the truth, or that a lie somehow makes you look better. A fat tomato for every lie you tell.

Hiding earns you a whopper of a tomato. You hide by refusing to take charge of your life. You're a constant victim of bad feelings and being afraid. You skip school, don't do homework, stay home, blob-out in front of the TV, get into trouble. You're blind to the truth that you're a terrific person with great potential.

Pretending is a waste of time because no matter how hard you pretend, you still have to face yourself and your circumstances. Pretending is to make-believe—and it's meant to deceive. When you were little, you pretended you were an astronaut or a scientist or a movie star and that was fun. Today if you pretend, be sure it's on the stage, not in real life where it's meant to deceive.

Quitting is not for you, because God never quits, never gives up. And most of all, He never gives up on you. He calls you His child and lavishes love on you. (If you don't *think* about being loved, you won't *feel* loved.) God will never give up on you, so how come *you* want to give up? Words like, "I don't feel like going to History class," or "I don't feel like going to the gym and working out," or "I don't feel like getting out of bed" are all quitter words.

God is telling you today—this very minute: "If you don't want spaghetti sauce on your face, stop throwing tomatoes at yourself!" You're too special.

You can change things. You can make your life better,

and you can stop depending on somebody else to do it for you. List right now some things you'd like to change and how you're going to do it.

TODAY

Make spaghetti sauce of your misbeliefs.

I thank you, Jesus, that you give me the power to change things and the mind of Christ to know what is mine to change. I don't want to continue throwing tomatoes at myself by lying, pretending, hiding and quitting. What a rut! Thank you for lavishing your love on me, for letting me be your child. You are always there to help me. Thanks.

Chapter 25

What If?

Don't you hate being miserable? I do. The best way I know to be miserable is to be afraid. Another way is to doubt God's love. Or doubt His word. The thing that turns misery into a heart full of joy and gladness is trust.

Let's play the *What If Game* just to check out our trust level. One of the tried and proven avenues to misery is the belief, *"I should get what I want."* Another sure-shot for Miseryville is the thought, *"Things should go the way I want them to."*

What if you really *did* get everything you wanted, and what if things always did go the way you wanted them to?

What if?

To play the *What If Game*, you have to check out these misbeliefs. For instance, what if you

In that day they will say, "Surely this is our God; we trusted in him, and he saved us. This is the Lord, we trusted in him; let us rejoice and be glad in his salvation."

Isaiah 25:9

told everybody you know that you should always get your own way? How would you feel as you demanded everybody give you your own way? What kind of things would you do to show them you must have your way? What reaction do you think you'd get from your friends? Your family?

Next, what if you only *thought* you should always get your own way but didn't actually tell anybody that? What if you told yourself you absolutely couldn't stand it if you didn't get your own way, but you kept quiet about your feelings? How would you feel inside? What kind of things would you do? How would your friends and family react?

Or, what if you believed deep down that everybody should like you? What if you told yourself nobody should ever dislike you or hurt you? How would this thought make you feel? What kind of things would you do? How would your friends and family react to the way you behaved? What if you find out somebody you thought was a friend really doesn't like you? What if you find out there are lots of people who don't like you?

When Jesus lived on earth, he always talked about the wonderful potential and abilities we have in Him. It's awesome to read how much promise and power the Bible tells us we have as Christians. "If anybody abides in me, he can ask what he wants and it will be done," He said.

What if you lived as if Jesus' words are true?

What if you saw yourself as Jesus sees you?

What if you really understood how precious you are to God?

What if you trusted the Lord so completely that you felt totally joyful in all situations and circumstances, even if they were difficult?

What if you *stopped* demanding that nothing go wrong and that everything be the way you want it to be?

What if the Lord Jesus gave you a big hug right now and told you He loves you and He's got great things ahead for you?

TODAY

Think of ten wonderful things about the Lord.

Dear Jesus, you never change. You always love me. You always care and show me the way. You always help me out of trouble and you always watch over me. I drop my urge for everybody's approval now in your name. I also drop my demands that I get my own way and that things always go the way I want them to. I release myself into your care and keeping now. I release myself from making harsh demands on people. I release myself to love the way you love. Amen.

Chapter 26

Changing Your Feelings

If it snowed today you might react with a shout of delight (unless, of course, you live in Florida). Someone else might react differently than you. He might have an unhappy response to snow—feelings of anger, sadness, fear. Each person responds differently.

Can you explain why so many different responses? The snow is exactly the same, but the people are not, you say. Yes, we're all different, but in what way?

We feel differently because we *think* differently. One of your friends, for example, might think how much fun it would be to play in the snow, so his reaction to snow is a happy one. Another friend might be angry at the snow, thinking that he will be forced to shovel the sidewalk now. Wor-

I the Lord search the heart and examine the mind.
Jeremiah 17:10

riers might be telling themselves that there will be more accidents and their bus could slide off the road on the way to school.

Listen to what you tell yourself and you will understand your feelings. Your feelings will change if your thoughts change. If you don't believe me, try this exercise: Imagine someone bumping into you and practically knocking you down. Your immediate response is anger. "Watch where you're going!" you snap. But suddenly you notice the person is blind.

Immediately you feel guilty. Sad.

There are four steps your mind takes on its way to your outward reaction. It works like this: (1) something happens to you; (2) you think about what happened; (3) the thoughts you have lead to a feeling; and (4) the feeling affects how you react. Let's slow down your collison.

What happened?	What did you think about it?	What did you feel?	What did you do?
Someone bumped into me.	It's rude to bump into somebody. It's thoughtless and hostile—like maybe the person is trying to start a fight.	Angry. Defensive.	Yelled.

True, it all happens in a split second. But what you tell yourself dictates your feelings.

TODAY

Work through the four steps in this devotion until it is clearly and soundly planted in your mind. Memorize Proverbs 19:8.

Thank you, Father, for making me totally different from every other person in the whole world. Thank you for showing me the tremendous power there is in our thoughts, and how important it is that I think your thoughts. Teach me to think your thoughts, Lord. I am really understanding now that happiness and success are in the way we think. Search my heart, Lord, and examine my mind. I want to be like you. Amen.

Chapter 27

Do You Believe God?

Have you memorized Proverbs 19:8 yet? You'll be glad you did when you're tempted to put yourself down.

This verse says if you gain wisdom you will be at peace with yourself. Wisdom, to me, means that you have three vital abilities: The ability to *hear* from God— "My sheep listen to my voice" (John 10:27); the ability to *believe* what He says is true—"Then the man said, 'Lord, I believe,' and he worshiped [Jesus]" (John 9:38); the ability to *act* on what He says—"Do not merely listen to the word, and so deceive yourselves. Do what it says" (James 1:22).

Gideon, in the Bible, was a man who needed wisdom. He was a farmer, and one day he was threshing wheat by hand in the bottom of a pit, where grapes

He who gets wisdom loves his own soul; he who cherishes understanding prospers.

Proverbs 19:8

were pressed to make wine, because he was fearful and hiding from the enemy, the Midianites.

Suddenly, without warning, an angel of the Lord appeared to Gideon and said, "The Lord is with you, mighty warrior."

Now, how would you feel if you were Gideon? Here he is, hiding in the bottom of a pit, afraid the Midianites will steal the family wheat—and an *angel* shows up telling him he is a mighty warrior.

Some shock, huh?

If an angel appeared to you and called you a mighty warrior, would you agree and respond, "That's right, I *am* a mighty person of valor. I am a mighty warrior because the Spirit of Christ lives in me and, like the Apostle Paul, in my weakness, Christ makes me strong. *Lord, I believe.*"

God called Gideon, an obscure farmer, to save Israel from being destroyed by the Midianite armies who desolated the country and made life intolerable.

Gideon argued with God: "But Lord, how can I save Israel? My clan is the weakest in Manasseh, and I am the least in my family" (Judges 6:15). Gideon had a real tough time thinking of himself as a mighty warrior, a military hero. He fussed, bargained and acted in fear, always thinking the opposite of what God was telling him.

It took a long time and a lot of work on God's part to convince Gideon that when God speaks, it is always true. God cannot lie. When He called Gideon a mighty warrior, He spoke *truth*. God made him a mighty warrior. Gideon thought he was supposed to be one in his own natural strength. He didn't understand God. He lacked wisdom.

Finally, Gideon caught on. Instead of doubting and acting like a nervous wreck, he gave his heart to God, lifted up his arms and worshiped Him by accepting the truth.

God's thoughts became his thoughts and he shouted to his men the words that the Lord had been telling him all along: "Get up! The Lord has given the Midianite camp into your hands" (Judges 7:15).

Gideon obeyed God and everything He said came true. The Midianites lost the war and never recovered. Israel enjoyed peace for forty years.

And so Gideon gained wisdom. The Word of God is true. What is He telling you today? Can you hear Him? Will you believe Him? Will you act on what He says?

Hearing God, believing Him and acting on His word gives you confidence and self-esteem. When you get wisdom—that is, when you continue on in what God teaches you in His Word—you will prosper in all you do and you will find good in your life.

TODAY

Read the story of Gideon in Judges
Chapter 6—8:32.

Yes, Lord, I will respond to your Word by believing and acting on it. I won't doubt or argue. I want to gain wisdom, Lord. Right at this very moment I give you my heart and mind for your Spirit to control and guide. Amen.

Chapter 28

The Winner's Circle

A lot of teenagers tell me they've never done anything really terrific with their lives. Sometimes I can tell what a guy or girl is going to say before either one says it.

"I know, I know," I interrupt. "You've never won a contest, never received an award, never been outstanding in anything. You feel like a lion in a world of Daniels. You've never been asked to give a speech, never gotten a plaque for being a team member, and never even received a perfect attendance button. Everybody else gets all the breaks and you're just doomed to live the lifestyle of the poor and obscure."

A ninth-grade boy named Carl almost had himself convinced he was the world's biggest loser. I tried to cheer him up by telling him to create some contests of his

What is more, I consider everything a loss compared to the surpassing greatness of knowing Christ Jesus my Lord, for whose sake I have lost all things. I consider them rubbish, that I may gain Christ and be found in him.

Philippians 3:8

own so he would be sure to win. So what did he do? He organized an all-school Cracker Crumbling Contest in the cafeteria on a day they were serving soup, figuring it was a sure win for him. When it came to cracker crumbling he was one of the best.

Carl told me how his hopes were dashed when he lost to a big-fisted, tenth-grade girl who pulverized her saltines and then wowed the audience by slurping down her cream-of-tomato in four gulps. Carl was depressed for a week.

Oh sure, I know it's neat to win something—to excel.

I believe in achieving. But when you put yourself under incredible pressure and make impossible demands on yourself to win, you're going to be unhappy.

If you're hard on yourself about winning and not winning, you'll be unhappy even when you win, because you will have taught yourself how to be unhappy and stressed out instead of how to be happy in all things. It's more important to teach yourself to be at peace and to be a person of contentment than it is to win contests.

I'm sure you've heard the old folk song and story of John Henry, the steel-driving man. He was famous for being a powerful man and the best steel driver on the railroad. Then one day a steam-powered, steel-driving engine was introduced, and everybody knew it would take the place of men who drive steel with a hammer all day. John Henry challenged the thing to a contest to see who could drive the steel stakes fastest.

John Henry, with incredible brute strength, actually won the contest and drove more stakes faster than the steam-powered engine. But he dropped dead of a heart attack before he could hear the crowd cheering.

Sometimes we put more energy into trying to prove ourselves than we do in seeking God's best for our lives. We get out of the winner's circle. A true winner is a person who, like the Apostle Paul, says "... that I may win Christ." Winning Him, being found in Him, knowing Him and the power of His resurrection is the greatest thing on earth. Anything else is losing.

TODAY

Ask yourself what you want to win—
and why.

*F*ather, I count all things as loss except the greatness of knowing you. I want to win you, know you, have you, live in you—and live in the Winner's Circle. Amen.

Chapter 29

Jesus Is Our Perfect One

I think I'll start a club and call it Perfectionists Anonymous.

But in order to belong to the club, you would have to promise to show up at all the meetings late and looking terrible, to do at least one thing badly each month, and to lose, drop, break, step on or goof up at least one important item during the course of a semester.

The girl who wrote me the following letter is definitely a candidate for the club.

Dear Marie:

In order for me to be an acceptable person, do I have to be perfect? Am I supposed to be a perfect student, perfect friend, perfect daughter, perfect everything?

My mom and dad tell me I should never be satisfied with my work or what I do because there's

God made him who had no sin to be sin for us, so that in him we might become the righteousness of God.

2 Corinthians 5:21

99

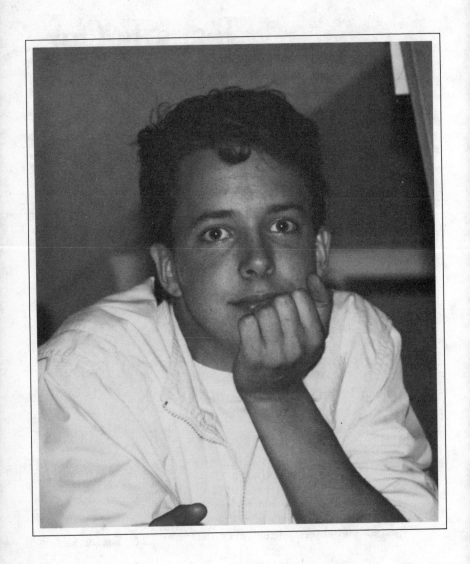

always room for improvement. They say I should always be concentrating on how to be *better.*

I don't think I can take it. I'm starting to hate school. I already hate studying. I'm so stressed out trying to be perfect that my grades are going down instead of up. Sometimes I don't even know what I'm studying. Is my mind going?

I lose my temper and blow up at friends. My parents took me to a psychologist who gave me some tests, and my I.Q. test showed I'm above average. I don't feel above average at all.

I feel like a walking time bomb. All I do is study, study, study. My only way out of all this pressure is to get sick. Sometimes I pray for the flu. I better end this letter. I have a paper to write and lots of homework staring me in the face. Do I sound like a crazy person to you? Help!

Signed,
Stressed out, worn out, burnt out and tuned out.

Dear S.O., W.O., B.O., and T.O.:

I'm aghast. No wonder you think your mind is going and you're praying for the flu. What awful pressure you live with! I had to do relaxation exercises just to get through your letter.

I name you Perfectionist of the Year. What's with you—may I call you S.O. for short? At the rate you're going, you'll never get one bite of the chicken kiev at your senior banquet. You know why? We'll all be visiting you as you lie on your sickbed surrounded on all sides by unfinished homework assignments and unopened books. You'll be gazing vacantly at the wall mumbling things like, "I got three wrong on that test and I studied so *hard!* What's wrong with me?"

You're too hard on yourself. Your demands are unfair and not very loving. You leave no room for "average" in your life.

Jesus is our perfect one. We can't be perfect in the sense that we *always* do 100 percent. We can be perfect in Him because He is perfect and becomes our righteousness (goodness, cleanness, rightness). But when you push yourself to excellence beyond what's required of you, you lose your joy in accomplishing anything at all. Learning won't be fun, achieving won't be fun, growing and discovering won't be fun. It's all so stressful!

As Perfectionist of the Year you're required to get at least one C before you're off the hook and you can hand in your shabby paper crown for your button, which reads, FREE TO BE AVERAGE.

Love,
A former perfectionist and charter member of P.A.

TODAY

Ease up. You're doing fine.

Set me free from "perfectionist" demands on myself, Lord. I know they are not of you. You are the Perfect One, the 100 percent righteous One. I do not wish to be a stressed-out child of God. Help me to release my fears and worries and these awful pressures in my life. Show me how, Lord. Amen.

Chapter 30

Ten Years of Piano Lessons and I'm Still Playing Scales

When I was in high school I wanted to be a cheerleader more than anything. To me, being a cheerleader was somewhat akin to being Miss America or Queen of England. I worked hard and practiced and finally faced the auditions.

It was a Mary Lou Retton harvest. Every girl leaped like Barishnakov and looked like a Hollywood starlet. I was shocked. When it came my turn to audition, I was so intimidated that I prayed to get a feverish cold so I could go home.

But I performed my routine, and surprisingly enough I made it. I was a cheerleader and I had the sweater to prove it. OK so I was a substitute, but I was a *cheerleader*.

My big debut was made on a

Let us not become weary in doing good, for at the proper time we will reap a harvest if we do not give up.

Galatians 6:9

bitter cold Minnesota night at a hockey game where I cheered my heart out on the ice.

Gymnastics didn't come easy for me. Acrobatics just weren't my "thing." (I always disliked the idea of being upside down and possibly landing that way.) But the sheer challenge of it drew me. The other cheerleaders could fly through the air doing their amazing, gravity-defying feats, and I doggedly labored at matching their skills. I cartwheeled, flipped, somersaulted, leaped, but never did I become the acrobatic *cause celebré* I longed to be.

The same was true of the piano. I had wonderful dreams for me and the piano. But I stopped my lessons.

Take inventory of your dreams now. Make a list of them. Once you have your list in front of you, recognize those things that will help your dreams come true and then also recognize the dream robbers.

Dream-come-true helps:

- Daily prayer and commitment to your dream for the glory of God. (If your dream doesn't glorify the Lord, you need to reevaluate.)
- Daily work and effort spent toward your goal. (Lessons, practice, studying, work.)
- Enthusiasm. (Remember, what you lack in talent, you can make up for at this point with your enthusiasm.)
- Love. Genuine love for what you are doing. If you don't love your dream, you'll give it up.

Dream robbers:

- Getting too "serious." Purpose daily to keep the joy in your dream. Joylessness is exhausting.
- Comparison thinking. If you compare yourself, your talents, skills, progress, with others, you'll become disheartened, frustrated and finally quit. Only compare yourself with yourself! The Lord Jesus and the

104

Word of God are your measuring devices, not some-body else who is working toward the same goal you are.

- No rewards. I know plenty of people who are hard on themselves, but I don't know many who have learned the skills of self-reward. Be sure to be good to yourself. Tell yourself things like, "Great job!" "You did that well!" "Good for you!"
- Overkill and imbalance. If you work at something fifteen hours a day, you're overdoing, of course; but if you work at something to the exclusion of all else, your heading for burn-out. Maybe now, maybe later. It doesn't matter when, although sometimes it happens just as you're about to attain the goal you've worked so hard for. Like the musician I know who threw a brilliant career down the tubes at the very height of his genius. He simply burned out. The work had become joyless, loveless and nonreward-ing. His life had become a torrent of imbalance and harsh self-demands.

TODAY

Give yourself time to play the scales of
life. Enjoy them.

Dear Lord Jesus, keep a tight hold on my ambitions and dreams. I give them to you to guide and nurture spiritu-ally. I will give my very best energies and work at devel-oping my skills and talents, but, Lord, keep me from being too hard on myself. Keep me from the dream robbers. Amen.

Chapter 31

Imperfect and Loving It

God is perfect. He takes care of us and protects us because we trust Him as our source of strength. *He* is the perfect, flawless One. We fall short and that's why we need Him.

An OK person knows that when the Bible tells us to "be perfect . . . as [our] heavenly Father is perfect" (Matt. 5:48), it doesn't mean we can't ever get a grade lower than an A.

Being perfect also does not mean you can never ever look bad, make a dumb mistake, or feel rotten. These little inconveniences of life simply show us our need of a Savior. (In order to be a member in the Perfectionists Anonymous club, you must repeat the previous two sentences five times every single day.)

Let's be honest. No matter

As for God, his way is perfect; the word of the Lord is flawless. He is a shield for all who take refuge in him.

Psalm 18:30

how old you are, sooner or later you're going to have to study *something*. School is a necessity of life. Learning and becoming good at something is an inevitable fate. Studying can be a lot of fun, and before you throw this book against the wall and yell ("Fun? Say *what*?"), let me ask you a few questions:

What do you think about the importance of studying hard? (A big "boo" to you if your answer is, "To achieve good grades.")

Do you think people who get good grades are brainy and smart? (Another big "boo" to you if your answer is yes.)

Do you think getting less than the highest scores and grades makes you inferior, less brainy, less smart?

Do you feel guilty when you don't get A's?

Are you embarrassed to tell anyone when you get a C or lower?

Have you ever given up something because you couldn't do as well as someone else?

If you answered yes to these last five questions, you are a person who does not enjoy studying. You're probably uptight about certain subjects at school because they're tough and you don't think you can do well in them. You may even be questioning your abilities to get into college. It's possible that you avoid doing homework until the very last minute. You may oversleep, watch TV, go out with your friends, talk on the telephone—anything to avoid the stress of studying.

But I meant it when I said studying can be fun. I've been going to school all my life. I can't remember not having a book under my nose. The words, "I can't talk now, I'm studying for finals," are more familiar to me than "Merry Christmas." Studying is fun only when it isn't stressful. The only way studying won't be stressful to you is when you change your drive to get top grades to possessing a new goal: *to have fun studying.*

Change your misbelief that brainy and smart people

get good grades because that means if *you* don't get good grades, you're brainless. (It's a bold-faced *lie!*)

Change your guilt-inducing self-talk when you don't get A's. Say, "Good for me. I studied hard. I could get to like this subject. Next time I will relax even better because I will feel better about myself."

Change your silly idea that if you aren't terrific at something, you ought to quit. Say, "Good for me. Here I am sticking with something I'm not great at. What character. What integrity. I'm no wimp."

The truth is: It's OK to be average. It's even OK to fail. It's OK to be imperfect. God tells us He is the perfect One, and in Him we are perfect and we are safe. Nobody is going to gouge out your toenails or slash your tires if you don't get straight A's. Your cousin Lenny may drive a Porsche and live a straight-A life, but that's *his* life. Let *him* live it. You live yours.

Chances are, when you start living your own life in Christ the way you were born to, your grades will go up and you'll be that achiever you would like to be. But it will be without pressure and stress!

TODAY

Reward yourself for doing your homework.

Thank you, Lord, for the refuge and shield you are to me against stress. Thank you that as a Christian I can be saved from the fear of failure and I can understand why studying can be so difficult. Thank you for showing me how studying can be fun. Amen.

Chapter 32

So She's Better Looking—But Is She Really *Happy?*

Can you imagine life without sarcasm, put downs or grumbling? Imagine what it would be like to never put down a friend. Or to make fun of someone. (One girl told me that without these things she'd practically have to give up life.)

Imagine never carrying a grudge about something that happened yesterday and never worrying about what will happen tomorrow. (A guy I know told me if he couldn't worry about the future, he would have nothing at all to think about.)

Thinking and worrying are two different things. And wanting to be liked is not the same thing as wanting to be better than others.

The way to truly glorify the Lord is to see yourself as a blessed

Ascribe to the Lord the glory due his name. Bring an offering and come before him; worship the Lord in the splendor of his holiness.

1 Chronicles 16:29

and "together" person. When you are happy with yourself, you'll discover you won't be so negative in your thinking. Your misbeliefs will not rule you as they once did. But it all starts in your thinking.

Do you ever entertain misbeliefs like: He or she "is better looking than I"; "isn't half as talented as I am"; "is jealous of me and can hurt me?"

Counteract those self-destructive statements with the truth: "I will *not* compare. I am *not* a Comparison Person." "I can appreciate every person's talent, including my own." "No one can hurt me unless I let them."

Our Bible verse for today speaks of bringing an offering to the Lord. Think of your offering today as bringing Him your mind, purified and filled with praise and love for Him and with thoughts of contentedness—that is, without complaints.

TODAY

Offer the Lord a twenty-four-hour day without once comparing yourself to somebody else. Give the Lord twenty-four hours of not comparing what you own, how you look, or what you do with what anybody else owns, looks like, or does.

Heavenly Father, be Lord of my thoughts today. I bring you the offering of a peaceful mind. I will not compare myself with anyone else today. I take your Spirit, pure and undefiled, into my own, and choose to refuse and rebuke unholy thoughts and words. Amen.

Chapter 33

Taking Revenge on Lenny

There you are, slumped over in your chair, staring at the stack of books on your desk. You've got a big paper due in two days and you haven't decided your topic. Besides, you have a huge Spanish test tomorrow and you haven't even looked at the vocabulary yet; there's your English Lit time-line, chapter 25 in your Algebra book plus the exercises at the end—and tonight's the game. Tomorrow you've got choir and youth group.

You slump farther in your chair. Suddenly you're horrifically tired. If you don't sleep you'll turn into a crawly monster. You'll do the homework later. Now you *must* get under the covers.

Suddenly your mother pops into the room, a clouded look on her face. "Have you done your homework?"

How great is your goodness, which you have stored up for those who fear you, which you bestow in the sight of men on those who take refuge in you.

Psalm 31:19

"I'm working on it."

"Those books have cobwebs on them!"

"Well, I'm *thinking*."

"What could you possibly be thinking about? Certainly nothing found on the pages within those crusty books. Another week on your desk and they'll be antiques."

"Mom, I think I'll take the shortest of naps—just a couple of winks so I can wake up real fresh and able to concentrate on all this homework."

"That's what you said yesterday. And the day before that. And last week. All you do is sleep!"

"I think it's my bones, Mom, They're growing so fast I'm exhausted. My brain can't keep up with the rest of me. I'm suffering an adolescent-growth-spurt crisis."

Your mother's face is reddening now. "I don't understand you. You're just throwing your life down the drain, wasting all your God-given intelligence and . . ." (Your mind wanders to what's on TV. It'll be time for supper soon. You'll need your nourishment for all this homework and mental harassment.) Your mother is now silent, glaring at you with a squinty right eye.

"Huh?" you say, trying to be funny. Now she's saying something like don't think you're going out tonight. "And don't try to pull any funny business with your dad either because it won't work. And why can't you be more like your cousin Lenny, the doctor?"

You stare dismally at the books. They're still there. Your mother tells you she is praying for you. There must be a better way to get through school than by studying.

You think of your cousin, the doctor. You and Lenny used to play together as little kids and he always cried when you won and he didn't. Suddenly you get a mental picture of cousin Lenny. He's smirking at you from behind the wheel of a shiny new Porsche while you're sitting on the curb caressing your only means of transportation—a pin-striped skateboard from Sears.

Your mother's prayers must have worked. You're inspired. Motivation floods your being. You're alive, alert. You feverishly attack the books, steam through the algebra assignment, outline the English paper and memorize two pages of irregular Spanish verbs. Never mind the game tonight. Who needs dinner? No way is Dr. Swamp Breath going to get the best of *you*.

As we fade out on this dramatic tableaux, let me ask you if you detected any misbeliefs in what you just read.

What motivates you? Are you motivated by competition? Do you have a cousin Lenny in your family? Do you get steamed at the thought of all the Lennys in this world who are achieving smugly and effortlessly while you're groaning at the thought of a mere book report?

God tells us He is a *good* God, not a competitive one. He is not telling us to get out there and smear, outdo, clobber, show up, wipe up, or compete against anybody. He tells us that in Him we can do all things. His goodness is so great He can make a terrific student out of you without your needing the motivation of competition.

Striving will wear you out.

Jealousy, anger and fear will wear you out.

Laziness will wear you out.

But the goodness of the Lord will flood you with delight in who you are, what you can do, and where you're at in Him.

He's proud of you.

TODAY

Pray for Lenny.

114

*D*ear Lord, I am going to stop avoiding homework and everything else in my life that seems hard. I know it's because I'm afraid I won't do well. I am giving that fear to you now, Lord. Your goodness is great and you deliver me from all my fears. Thank you for taking anger and a striving spirit from me. Amen.

Chapter 34

Can Anxiety Be Fatal?

*T*rudy, a bright girl of sixteen was suffering a gigantic anxiety attack and couldn't face her homework, so she wrote a letter instead:

Dear Marie:

I think I have a deep-seated self-hatred. I can think of a million other things to do besides my homework, including eat, sleep, talk on the phone, bake cookies for my friends and even type my boyfriend's papers. Take last night for instance. I stayed up till 2 a.m. typing a history paper for him, and my own homework sat on my desk untouched. I had Geometry class first thing this morning, and I didn't hand in the assignment. I must hate myself pretty bad, huh? Do you think I have a hidden urge to fail, or to self-destruct?

Please tell me what's wrong with me. Is there hope for a per-

I sought the Lord, and he answered me; he delivered me from all my fears. Those who look to him are radiant; their faces are never covered with shame.

Psalm 34:4, 5

son who will even stoop so low as to clean her room to get out of working on a term paper?

Signed,
Moping Not Coping

P.S. My parents weren't good students, either, and my dad is a high school drop out. Both my parents had to go to work to help out their parents. Does this mean anything?

Dear M.N.C.:

Cheer up, kid, you don't hate yourself. You just hate homework. Stop trying to come on neurotic and bonkers when all you have is a morbid dislike for cracking those books. I must tell you, I've heard some pretty hairy stories in my time, but *cleaning your room* to get out of something is sinking real low.

Since you are a person who seems to hate homework, you must—must—*must* use these SUCCESS TECHNIQUES FOR THOSE WHO DESPISE HOMEWORK. Here they are:

Face the problem. Tell yourself, "I'm going to build a protective bubble around me so that nothing upsets or worries me until I get my homework done."

Get fortified. When you start to nervously fidget with your pen and pull hairs out of your head, say out loud, "I am more than a conquerer. I am a person who will not stay in a rut. I will not be a victim of anxiety and hatred of homework!"

Focus your attention. Tell yourself, "I will pay attention to the assignment. I will make a list of steps to take in this assignment and do one at a time until I am finished."

Cope, don't mope. Pay close attention to your feelings as you work. Be a friend to yourself, and when you recognize negative thoughts creeping into your mind, tell yourself, "Whoops, I'm starting to get worried about doing this assignment right. I know if I relax, focus on the work and save the evaluating until later, I'll do OK. *I can do all things through Christ who strengthens me.*" Coping means breathing deeply and relaxing.

117

Reward yourself. Tell yourself, "Hey, that's great! I finished that part of the assignment. I did it without getting uptight. I didn't pull out my hair. I didn't go to the bathroom or go get something to eat. I stayed with it. I did it!"

Love,
An Anxiety Survivor
and Your Friend

P.S. It's OK to do better in school than your parents did.

TODAY

Copy the five points of the *Where-It's-At Success Techniques for Those Who Hate and Despise Homework and Schoolwork in General* and keep them with you always. Carry them in your notebook, tack them on your bulletin board, tape them inside the lining of your jacket—remember them.

Father, I will remember who I am in Christ Jesus and that homework does not have to be drudgery, even if my parents hated it. Even if my cousin Lenny is better at it than I. Even if it's hard and I might not get terrific grades. Even if I don't feel very smart. I won't die of anxiety. I can handle it. I can learn to reward myself for what I do well and for just plain doing—even if I don't do it perfectly. Forgive me, Lord, for thinking rewards are only for the perfect. Amen.

Chapter 35

The Place Called Home

*I*t seems to me—correct me if I'm wrong—that there's a Mc-Donald's restaurant everywhere on this planet. I was watching the sports segment of the 6 o'clock news the other night and an American soccer team was being filmed on a trip to Australia.

The camera showed our guys strolling along the streets of Sidney, looking in the shop windows, gazing at tall buildings, and then, to their amazing, wondering eyes, there appeared—the golden arches!

"C-could that be Mc-Donalds?" asked one incredulously.

"Wouldn't it be *something* if it was McDonalds?" the other crowed.

Their pace quickened. They walked faster toward the vision

For in the day of trouble he will keep me safe in his dwelling; he will hide me in the shelter of his tabernacle and set me high upon a rock.

Psalm 27:5

119

before them. Then they were running. "It is! It is! *Mc-Donald's!*"

The next shot showed the entire team hovering over heaps of paper-wrapped Mcburgers, Mcfries, Mcsodas and Mcshakes.

"Just like home," grinned one of them as he munched a Mcnugget. He was ecstatic. I was Mcshocked.

The mere sight of the golden arches gave these guys a feeling of *home*. A hamburger provided a sensation of security.

When I was going to school in New York City and away from home for the first time, I'd get those same feelings when I passed a church, any church. I often stopped on my way somewhere to duck into a church and just sit on a pew in the silence all alone. A church felt like *home*, like security—love. Fast-food restaurants didn't do for me what those majestic city churches did.

Is there a place that gives you a sense of security, of belonging, of peace? Maybe it's your room, or your old neighborhood, or your grandma's kitchen—your car.

The Lord Jesus has a place for you called "home." It's a safe place where you're perfectly protected and cherished. It's better than any McDonald's and better than a city church—it's within His heart. *That's* your true home.

"In my father's house are many mansions," He said. In His heart there is a dwelling place for you. That's where you belong—in His care. That's where you're safest and where you'll be happiest.

As a Christian take your rightful place in Him and talk to Him about it.

TODAY

Jesus wants you to have the feeling of security and love with Him only. At the mention of His name you feel at home. All else in your life is a result of this security in the Lord and His love for you.

Thank you, Jesus, for giving me a true home in you and no matter where I might travel in this world, I am at "home" because I am always with you, and you will never leave me nor forsake me. Thank you for such a deep and happy sense of safety and security. Amen.

Chapter 36

Church Is Where It's At

*H*ere's Clayton Farnsby sitting in 10th-grade Math doing his Spanish homework. Clayton is feeling down-in-the-dumps today. In fact, you might say he is totally flippo.

Clayton is a Christian and has been born again since he was just a tot. He says he loves the Lord but sometimes he feels twinges of jealousy. When he hears thrilling testimonies of death-defying salvations or thrills-and-chills Christian stories, his own pales in ordinaryness.

Clayton figures that growing a beard may solve his problems. But in two weeks no hairy shadows have appeared on his face. Clayton is slipping downward toward the pit of worldly rottenness. He is a victim of what I call *The Nasty Non-Fellowship Blues.*

Better is one day in your courts than a thousand elsewhere; I would rather be a doorkeeper in the house of my God than dwell in the tents of the wicked.

Psalm 84:10

Some of his symptoms include a crush he has on a girl who is not a Christian; he's swearing and using vulgar words more and more lately, he's sullen and nasty at home, and he watches tons of TV.

The Nasty Non-Fellowship Blues are deadly. They can do you in faster than you can say, "Bye-bye, Clayton Farnsby!"

It all begins with cunning improvidence. Like taking a part-time job that requires you to work on Sundays and on youth night, or missing church to play tennis or do your English homework.

Does any of this ring a bell?

Dear God;

I sat down to write you a beautiful poem,
But my genius was interrupted by the phone.
I've decided to give you my life and my all,
But do you mind if I just take this call?

Well, I certainly feel that my prayer life is great;
I pray every night when I stay up late.
I'm a giver, a do-er, a true Jesus man,
And I even quote Scripture whenever I can.

I was raised in the church and I loved it, but then
I lost the excitement I had way back when.
Don't leave me out, Lord, I want to belong,
But will going to church really make me strong?

O Lord, to know you more and more!
Ooops, please excuse me, there's someone
    at the door.
I'm ready to serve you every day,
But the ball game is starting
And it's time to go play.

I wrote that little poem and handed it to Clayton. I wish I could tell you he fell on his knees in conviction and vowed to be in church every single Sunday for the

124

rest of his natural life, but Clayton remained a victim of The Nasty Non-Fellowship Blues for about a year before he turned around and recommitted his life to the Lord. In that year's time he lost out on more joy, more good things, more friendships and terrific experiences than he can count. He lamented his blindness to the truth, but finally accepted the forgiveness of the Lord and went on with his life.

There aren't enough words to express to you how absolutely *vital* it is for you to be involved in a church. I don't mean just as a person who sits there each week and then trucks on home. I'm talking *involved*. You need to love and be loved, serve God, be a blessing and get blessed. You will learn so much about the Lord, grow in Him, and worship Him with your whole life. Jesus says, "For where two or three come together in my name, there am I with them" (Matt. 18:20).

TODAY

Center your life around your church. Make sure you are there every Sunday, no matter what. Don't miss youth group. If your church doesn't have a youth group, find a good Bible-believing church that does have one. Include your family if you can. If your family doesn't want to go to church, don't use it as an excuse to stay home. *You* go.

Dear Lord Jesus, guide me to a Bible-believing church where I can worship you. I want to center my life around your church and I want to be a part of your family. Amen.

Chapter 37

Help Me, I Hurt!

Dear Diary

Today my dad moved out. He said he'd be back to see me and come to take me places on weekends. Carol and Kim came over and we played games on the computer. Kim is fat and wears big braces on her teeth. She has yukky, tweaked hair. Boys don't like her. But when her dad came to pick her up, I would have given anything to change places with her because she has a dad who loves her.

When my Dad's home it's a good feeling, like having a lock on the door. You feel safe, like he's there to be bigger than the rest of the world. Now it's just Mom and my little sister, Kerry, and me. It's quiet. Even with TVs and radios blaring, the house feels silent and still. When Mom talks to me I don't want to answer her.

So do not fear, for I am with you; do not be dismayed, for I am your God. I will strengthen you and help you; I will uphold you with my righteous right hand.

Isaiah 41:10

126

I'm sure it's all Mom's fault Dad left. Why wasn't she nice to him? She could have done something to make him stay with us. Maybe she shouldn't have cut her long hair, or maybe she should have gone on a diet. If mothers were perfect, fathers wouldn't get divorces. They would love their families. Why did Daddy find himself a girl-friend? I feel dumb now for the scene I made—begging him the way I did not to go. I'm such a freak.

Nobody could understand how I feel. Dad just stopped loving us, I guess. I don't think anyone on this earth will ever love me. If my own dad doesn't love me, why should anybody else? Personally, dear diary, *I don't care.*

The above diary entry is a real one. It was written by a fifteen-year-old girl. How did you feel when you read it? Do you think her feelings are justified? Do you think God has given up on her and her family?

Maybe you or somebody you know has gone through what she is experiencing. This fifteen-year-old has some very real hurts, and it's hard for her to feel God's love at this time.

One way we express hurt is to try to convince our-selves we don't care. When we say "I don't care," we are really saying we care so much it hurts.

When you feel hurts that seem to crush you into little pieces of dust, it's important to know God hears you. He sees your tears. He knows when you cry and He cares about what hurts you. He knows what it means to feel alone and rejected. He knows what it feels like to have the whole world drop out from under you.

Jesus knows and He holds out His warm, gentle and strong arms to catch you when you feel yourself falling. He will hold you tightly when you're in trouble.

TODAY

Reach out for the strength of the Lord
to hold you up if you hurt. Reach out
to someone else who may be hurting.

*F*ather, *I lift up my family and the families of my friends.*
Strengthen the relationships between mothers and fa-
thers. Bless the marriages and the homes so that families
are strong and happy. Touch my house with your love
and mercy, and bless my parents in your mighty name.
Amen.

Chapter 38

Don't Talk Me Out of My Feelings

*T*he girl we read about yesterday was angry with her mother. Do you think her anger seemed fair? She was angry because her mother couldn't keep her dad from leaving. She had begged her dad not to go.

But nobody should have to beg for love. Not the girl who wrote in her diary, not her mother, not you, not anybody. Love is a gift we give freely to each other with no strings attached. We are loved because we *are.*

She pleaded with God to make her parents love each other again, to change her dad's mind about leaving, to make him no longer interested in that other woman. And so far God hadn't answered the way she wanted Him to. She even felt God had turned His back on her.

Who shall separate us from the love of Christ? Shall trouble, or hardship, or persecution or famine or nakedness or danger or sword [or divorce]?

Romans 8:35

Do you ever feel God has turned His back on you? Such feelings are real and need to be expressed. Your feelings are important. Everyone should be able to cry and be angry without trying to hide true feelings.

Stuffing painful feelings is to hurt even worse. If you're hurting, don't be a feeling stuffer. Talk to someone. Let your feelings be expressed in words. Words like, "Here is how I feel . . ."

Pray and ask the Lord of Love to put you in touch with your own feelings. When you feel bad, ask Him to allow you to put your feelings into words and to express them to someone who won't judge you or try to talk you out of your feelings.

Be sure you are a *listener* when someone expresses his hurts to you, too. Don't offer advice, just be there. God is there, and if He cares, so can we. First of all, care enough yourself to realize that even though people may leave us, He *never* does. People may fail us, hurt us, reject us, but God *never* does.

You can never lose the Lord in a crowd, never lose Him in the sorrows of circumstances. Whether you're sleeping or awake, He is right beside you. The very hairs on your head are numbered, and He is holding you close to Him right now.

TODAY

Experience the closeness of the Lord. Concentrate and meditate on His nearness. Nothing can separate you from Him—nothing.

*F*ather, *heal my hurts. Hold me in your heart and help me to accept your love for me. No matter what happens in my life, whether rejection, failure, hurt or happy success, I am yours and my life is yours. Amen.*

Will God Ever Answer My Prayers?

Dear Diary

I can't understand why God doesn't answer my prayers. He just doesn't care, I guess. Fine. What do I care?

Today my mother is going to look for a job. That means I'll get stuck baby-sitting Kerry. Just great. She's such a brat when Mom's not around.

Dad said he'd come and get me and take me out this morning. He still hasn't showed up. I've been waiting a long time. He must have gotten delayed. When he comes I'm going to ask him if I can go live with him. I'll cook and even do the laundry. I won't be any trouble at all. Dear God, let him say yes.

Later—

It's noon and Dad still isn't here. Mom stuck me with Kerry, of course, so when Dad comes for me, I won't get to be alone with him.

Why are you downcast, O my soul? Why so disturbed within me? Put your hope in God, for I will yet praise him, my Savior and my God.

Psalm 43:5

Later later—
    Carol and Kim called but I said I couldn't go out. I didn't tell them my dad is coming.

Later later later—
    Dad didn't show and I'm going to bed now. Good night, diary, Sweet dreams. Ha. Ha. Try not to hate me, too.

It's been a year since this girl wrote those words in her diary. Today, she still lives with her mother and sister. Her dad still forgets to come when he says he will, and he often forgets to call. My young friend no longer cries and blames God (or her mother), though. Her life is as normal and happy as anyone else's her age. She has good friends, including Carol and Kim, and she has stopped feeling horrible and unloved.

This change and new growth didn't happen by accident. Contrary to the popular old saying, time does not heal all wounds. What heals wounds is the skillful application of the Word of God in your life. Jesus is the healer, not time. Jesus knows a lot about rejection.

When Jesus was praying in the garden of Gethsemane, He felt utterly abandoned by His disciples whom He asked to stand watch. They fell asleep instead of watching over Him.

On the cross Jesus was jeered at, insulted and jabbed at while agonizing and hanging by nails driven through His flesh. Nobody rallied on His behalf. No troops of soldiers rushed in to His defense. He was alone with a handful of followers mourning nearby.

Jesus is well-acquainted with feelings of despair. He was tempted to be miserable and feel defeated and rotten, but He conquered those feelings. The Bible says, "We do not have a high priest [Jesus] who is unable to sympathize with our weaknesses, but we have one who has been tempted in every way, just as we are—yet was without sin" (Hebrews 4:15).

That's why we call Him Savior and why we can approach His Father's throne with confidence that we'll receive mercy and find grace to help us in our time of need (Hebrews 4:16). Jesus overcame. Jesus conquered. He died on the cross to give us His Spirit to live in us so we, too, can conquer and overcome.

My young friend could have remained angry and bitter and hurt for many years. I've seen people who go on and on with their hurts as though every day the hurt is fresh and the pain of yesterday occurs all over again with each breath. It's tragic. It's a waste.

God wants to bless you today. He wants to give you His joyous heart. He wants to teach you the secret of laughing through your tears. He wants to wash you clean of hurts and pain with His precious blood.

TODAY

Allow the Lord to work in your heart with His healing, creative touch of love and power. He will wash out hurts and bitterness, no matter what the cause. Even if you've been wronged, give your feelings of anger and pain to Jesus. Tell Him, as Job did, "When He has tried me, I shall come forth as gold" (Job 23:10). God *is* answering your prayers. Never ever, ever give up. No matter how dark it looks, God answers.

Thank you, Lord, for answering me. Thank you for the truth that hurt does not last forever. Thank you, Lord, that you give me a time to hurt and a time to heal. Thank you for never leaving me in the pit of despair by showing me the way out. Thank you for being the way out of darkness and into life and freedom. I love you, and I choose to walk in love. Amen.

Chapter 40

Your Awesome Time With God

Can you hear the Lord talking to you? Can you hear His gentle, quiet voice calling your name?

The way to hear the voice of God is through a daily commitment to your prayer time. Call it your Awesome Time With God.

Nothing in this world will compare with it.

Each day (a terrific time is first thing in the morning) open your Bible for a short reading, and then pray. Praying is speaking to God.

When I pray I do five things. They are the first four of our Five Power Points:

Praise the Lord and worship Him.

Thank Him.

Intercede for others.

Ask and receive.

Some days praise and worship takes over my prayer time. Other

"For I know the plans I have for you," declares the Lord, ". . . plans to give you hope and a future. Then you will call upon me and come and pray to me, and I will listen to you. You will seek me and find me when you seek me with all your heart."

Jeremiah 29:11, 12

days, thanking Him may command most of my attention. Then still, at other times I intercede and pray for others and can think of nothing else but their needs. Last of all, there's asking and receiving. *Never beg.* The Bible says, "I was young and now I am old, yet I have never seen the righteous forsaken or their children begging bread" (Psalm 37:25).

You don't have to beg God. He hears you and He answers you. You can talk as loudly or as quietly as you like. You can jump up and down, or you can quietly sit in a chair. You can lie down or stand up. You can clasp your hands together with your fingers turned upward, or you can wave them in the air as you pray. It doesn't matter. He's not hard of hearing.

Isaiah 65:24 gives us a glimpse into God's heart: "And it shall come to pass, that before [you] call, I will answer; and while [you] are yet speaking, I will hear" (KJV).

Keep a prayer journal so you can write down what the Lord is showing you every day. Keep notes and prayer requests, answered prayer, and any communication you wish to enter.

Then there's a Fifth Power Point:

Listening to God.

The Word of God is a direct line to heaven. He will also speak to you in your heart. He speaks to you in your thoughts. It doesn't matter *how* you hear Him just hear Him! Know Him. He said, "My sheep hear my voice, and I know them, and they follow me" (John 10:27, KJV).

In Jeremiah, we read the story of a watchman at a gate. The watchman opens the gate for the shepherd and the sheep follow the shepherd through the gate. "The sheep *listen* to his voice. He calls his own sheep by name and leads them out" (John 10:3). Sheep follow their shepherd because they know his voice. They won't follow a stranger because they don't recognize the stranger's voice.

Jesus is telling you today, "Ask and it will be given to you; seek and you will find; knock and the door will be opened to you. For everyone who asks receives; he who seeks finds; and to him who knocks, the door will be opened" (Luke 11:9, 10).

TODAY

Commit yourself to daily prayer. Make a special place for yourself where you pray every day. (Even though you may dialogue with God all day long, you still need a special time and place that is set apart for just you and the Lord Jesus alone.) Keep your Five Power Points and expect your Awesome Time With God to be the most wonderful time of your entire day.

I worship you, Lord, I love you. I thank you. I thank you for the gift of prayer, for the sweet fellowship you and I have together. Thank you, Lord, for answering prayer, for caring, for loving and for being Lord of lords and King of kings and my Savior. Thank you for being my friend. Amen.

Chapter 41

Discovering the Meaning of Obedience

Arabian horses are not ordinary horses, they're special. They're a most expensive and highly-regarded horse, requiring expert training. If the Arabian horse does not pass the rigorous and demanding tests of training, it has little value. In fact, the horse is dangerous if it isn't made perfectly obedient through training. On the Arabian desert, for instance, if the horse is not 100 percent obedient to its master, it could cause his death.

In order for the Arabian horse to learn perfect obedience, it must pass each of the severe tests in its training. The worst of these tests is one the horse is put through right at the end of its training. The trainer withholds water from the horses until they are nearly dying of thirst. It's a horrible thing to be

But I gave them this command: Obey me, and I will be your God and you will be my people. Walk in the ways I command you, that it may go well with you.

Jeremiah 7:23

in the 130-degree desert heat and blinding sun for days on end without water.

While they're traveling, the trainer is leading them to water. As they draw near the water, the horses can smell it and they break loose with the last bit of strength in their weakened bodies. Just as they reach the edge of the water and are about to plunge in, the trainer blows his whistle to make them stop.

The cruelest act is actually a blessing! The horses that stop short without drinking and trot back to the trainer are the horses of greatest value, the prize horses. They are perfectly obedient.

Why is such a severe test of obedience necessary? Because a spirited, self-willed horse cannot serve its master well. All rebellion and disobedience has to go. A horse

doesn't know what's what. You wouldn't want to entrust your life to one who didn't obey. Trust is a key.

You and I have to *learn* to be trustworthy, too. There's a training we go through. Jesus said, "If anyone would come after me, he must deny himself and take up his cross daily and follow me" (Luke 9:23).

Even Jesus told the Father, "Not my will, but yours be done" (Luke 22:42). Jesus had to learn obedience to God exactly as you and I do. The Bible tells us, "Although he [Jesus] was a Son, he *learned* obedience from what he suffered" (Hebrews 5:8).

Jesus *learned* obedience. You and I *learn* obedience. Maybe He is teaching you the way the trainer taught his Arabian horses. Just when you think you can't take one more trial, just when you think you see the answer to all your problems before you and you're ready to plunge into the water, Jesus may blow the whistle.

What will you do?

TODAY

Listen for the Master's whistle.

Sometimes I am as wild as an Arabian horse. I need you as my divine trainer in order to walk in the ways you command me. I want to be the happy and blessed person you called me to be. I am willing to be trained. I am willing to hear the whistle. Amen.

Chapter 42

When God Blows the Whistle

*E*llen needed a part-time, after-school job. She felt desperate because her mother had been laid off from where she worked and the family had little money. She had prayed, her family had prayed, and she told God she wanted His perfect will in her life.

Ellen landed a job. She was ecstatic. Soon her mother could count on help. After two days Ellen realized she'd never see the paycheck her family so desperately needed. The atmosphere at her new job was oppressive and negative. Her co-workers constantly used obscene language. Ellen saw lying, dishonesty, drugs and rivalry.

At first she tried to close her eyes to what was going on. She even tried convincing herself it

Help me to do your will, for you are my God. Lead me in good paths for your Spirit is good.
        Psalm 143, TLB

141

was a good mission field. Maybe God put her there to win them all to Jesus. But she knew God was telling her otherwise when the boss began making a play for her. Ellen had no choice but to quit.

She felt horrible. She complained to her mother, "I don't understand it. I thought God gave me the job. I prayed for His *perfect* will, didn't I? The Lord knows I need a job. He knows how much we need the money. How could He allow me to make such a terrible mistake?"

Do you think Ellen was justified in feeling the way she felt?

How does God blow the whistle in your life to train you in a walk of perfect obedience?

TODAY

Tell yourself obedience sometimes hurts, but you are always safe in your Lord and Savior who loves you. He will always lead you the right way and on the right path because His Spirit is good.

Father, I know obedience is something I have to learn. I want to be obedient so I can be a prize servant in your kingdom. I put myself under your authority now. Whatever it takes, teach me. I am willing to turn from what I think looks good. I am willing to hear the whistle. Amen.

Chapter 43

Just Because I'm Not Paranoid Doesn't Mean They're Not Out to Get Me

*E*ver known someone who complains *all* the time? It's no blast to be with someone who is always complaining, fault-finding and putting someone or something down, is it?

I've met people who treat the world as if it were an enemy. They always seem to be struggling with invisible boogie men. In their minds, there's a problem or a threatening situation around every corner.

These chronic complainers think of sales people as thieves. They see all politicians as crooks. They carry vendettas for the telephone company, land developers, policemen, teachers, TV preachers, all rich people, and anyone who drives an exclusive European sportscar. They think "other" people get all the breaks

I have learned to be content whatever the circumstances. I know what it is to be in need, and I know what it is to have plenty. I have learned the secret of being content in any and every situation, whether well fed or hungry, whether living in plenty or in want.

Philippians 4:11, 12

143

and that somebody is always out to get them or take something away from them.

These people are b-o-r-i-n-g. You could fall asleep ten times during one of their tirades about the injustice of the curve-grading system. And you're really in trouble if you get trapped into listening to one of their speeches on how stupid college entrance exams are and how only a moron would find a computer hard to learn.

Once I was corralled into going to lunch with one of these chronic complainers. I sat dozing over my Caesar salad during a boring soliloquy on how rotten all her classes were, how there were absolutely *no* cute guys left in the world—when all of a sudden I was zapped with a *positive* note.

I was so stunned I nearly fainted in the lettuce. Her positive note was: "I guess I'll have to trust the Lord."

"How sensible," I gasped.

But that was the end of it. Every other word was negative, dreary, hopeless, morose and depressing. Never in my life was I so glad to see a check placed on the table. Before my friend could see the amount and complain about the prices in restaurants these days, I snatched it

up, plunked down money to cover the meal (including the tip), and smiled a warm, I'm-rushing-off smile. And rushed off.

You can be in the midst of trials, but you don't have to be strung out and wiped out, bummed out and tuned out. Refuse all tendencies to complain.

Tell yourself that you are a person who is learning to be *content* in all circumstances of life. Tell yourself you will enjoy being creative when you face trials and problems.

TODAY

Complain about absolutely nothing, including the weather. Tell yourself, "Surely goodness and mercy are following me" because the Word of God says so. Read Psalm 23 at least once.

Heavenly Father, I refuse to be a chronic complainer. Help me to recognize my tendencies to complain, find fault, or expect bad things to happen. Give me a hopeful, happy heart, Jesus—like you have. Amen.

Chapter 44

Good Things Are Happening to Me (Except for . . .)

Sometimes your biggest problems can live right in your own house! How do you get along with your brothers and sisters? They can be buddies or enemies, depending upon you. (Don't get all defensive now—read on.)

If you're not buddies with your brothers and sisters, it's because there are what I call "Buddy Busters" in your house. Here's a list of them:

Jealousy.
Competition.
Fighting.
Moodiness and being hard to
    get along with.
Not respecting each other's
    things.
Not respecting each other's
    friends.
Putting down what's impor-
    tant to each other.

The Lord will indeed give what is good.
                    Psalm 85:12

My command is this: love each other as I have loved you.
                    John 15:12

Making fun of each other's talents and skills.

Not encouraging each other.

Acting bossy and like a know-it-all.

Pride and being unwilling to say "I'm sorry" or "I was wrong."

Anger and temper tantrums.

Defensiveness and always insisting on having your own way.

Not taking enough time to do things together.

Not sharing equal responsibilities.

Not being thoughtful or kind to each other.

Impatience.

Making cruel and unkind jokes at the other's expense.

Not doing nice things for each other on a regular basis and being thanked for it.

Being rude or nasty to parents.

If you can check at least three of these Buddy Busters, you and your brother(s) and/or sister(s) could benefit by some caring and open communication.

You could pin the blame on your siblings, but resist the urge. Try to apply these gentle reminders to yourself first. Do *you* compete? Are *you* jealous? Are you overbearing and bossy? Do you fight and are *you* moody and hard to get along with?

Ouch.

Sorry. It really isn't "all his/her fault," even though I know it takes more than one person to have a fight and there ought to be a law against all brothers and sisters until they reach the age of two hundred or so. But what can you do? You're not an only child. It was God's way of humbling you, right?

So even though brothers and sisters can be stinky at times, think of it this way—you're somebody's brother or sister. And *you're* certainly not rotten, so there must be hope.

Start by wanting to have a good buddy who also happens to be a brother or sister. Now you're on your way to something terrific. Honest. I've watched families for a long time and I've noticed the people who fight as teenagers don't just miraculously become great friends later on in life. Many people I could name didn't get along with their brothers and sisters when they were growing up and still don't get along with them today. I think they're missing out. That's very sad.

It takes work and skill to be buddies with your brothers and sisters. First, you have to ask yourself, "Why do I want to be a buddy with my brother or sister?" Write that answer in a secret place in your heart. Then pray for wisdom and guidance as you begin to create a new relationship out of one that has been very uncreative.

My dad always told my brother and sister and me, "You kids are closer to one another than your mom and I are. That's because you have the same parents and the

same blood runs through your veins. You must remember and respect that. Nobody in the world will ever be as close to you as your brother or sister.''

That awareness wasn't always there when my sister was using my makeup or my brother was loaning my bike to his friends. But (you'll hate me for this) I must say I honestly cannot ever remember fighting with them. I can't ever remember a time when our parents had to tell us to stop arguing. We were told to be quiet and to stop running or playing so loudly in the house, but never to stop fighting. We just didn't fight.

TODAY

Talk to your brother(s) and/or sister(s) and make a quality decision to be buddies. Go over the Buddy Buster list together. Decide to care, be kind, listen, reward, encourage and befriend one another at home and away from home. If you do it now, you'll have a buddy forever.

Dear Lord Jesus, I release the power of the Holy Spirit in my home and upon the relationship I have with my brothers and sisters. I will not give in to the selfish attitudes that antagonize my brothers and sisters. I choose to eliminate the Buddy Busters that have been destroying our relationship. Amen.

Chapter 45

Good Things Are Happening to You

Good things are happening in your life right now—whether you think so or not. Count three good things that are happening right now and write them down. Call this your "Good Things Are Happening List," or your GTAHL. (Think how much time and energy you spend telling yourself how bad things are. What you'll be doing now is giving good things equal attention.)

Now you're ready to make another list. This one is your "I Won't Lose It List" (IWLIL).

Start you IWLIL by naming three things that could bring on a sudden relapse into the gloomy world of complaining and depression and possible despair. Example: Your older brother calls you a creep and makes you feel like a total airhead. Or your little sister

The Lord is good, a refuge in times of trouble.
Nahum 1:7

takes something of yours *again* without asking and then runs and tells your mother you're picking on her.

There is nothing like a clash with a brother or sister to ruin your GTAHL. There you are, sailing away on a wave of inner peace and outer joy and God sends you a brother or sister!

I know one teenager who has *seven* younger brothers and sisters. He told me it wouldn't be so bad if he didn't have to take care of them so much. By the time he finished telling me his horrible plight in life, I was convinced this poor guy did nothing but baby-sit twenty-four hours a day. "Who's watching them *now*?" I asked fearfully, looking around for seven short people. None in sight.

It turned out that the situation wasn't as bad as my friend had convinced himself it was.

When you make your IWLIL, you'll see that the very things you think cause you to lose your GTAH awareness aren't so horrible. (I have the feeling you don't believe me. Let's get on with our IWLIL strategy!)

Your IWLIL is very important because it's your strategy for Preparing for the Pittsville Attack. (You *know* how it feels to be in the Pitts, right? Well, Pittsville is even worse.) One minute you're feeling great and then your sister lays a heavy competitive trip on you and boom, it's Pittsville.

So you have to be *ready*. You don't want to lose it. After all, you've now learned how. You can handle it. You've arrived! Tell yourself what we've already learned in this book: *Things, situations, events and relationships are not what make me upset and unhappy—it's what I tell myself about these things that bring my response.*

You might write something like this on your IWLIL: "I'm in danger of losing it when: (1) my brother calls me a creep and an airhead; (2) my sister goes in my dresser drawers and takes something without asking; (3) I'm stuck baby-sitting for my brothers and sisters on Friday night.

Knowing what will tempt you to "lose it" prepares you

for the Pittsville attack. When it happens you counter-attack with your Good Things Are Happening List.

And ask yourself, "What is it I have to do when I'm facing a Pittsville attack?" Answer: "I'll think carefully and slowly and remind myself not to over-react." *Peace I leave with you; my peace I give you* (John 14:27).

TODAY

Tell yourself and the Lord, "I won't lose my happiness. My enemy is not my brother or sister. My enemy is not my parent or anyone else. I won't get stuck in Pittsville. I will tell myself the truth. Good things are happening to me!

Thank you, Jesus, for giving me good things! Thank you for showing me I don't have to lose my peace. Pittsville doesn't have to be threatening me every time I take another breath. I can control my life with you as my Savior and Lord—and with the Word of God as my guide—and with the Holy Spirit as my teacher, my Comforter, and my power. I am not going to lose it!

Chapter 46

How to Talk to Parents (Even When You Don't Want to)

*D*o you talk to your parents?

Maybe you're like Jeff who complains, "My parents *police* me all the time. When I walk out the door, it's, 'Where are you going?' 'Who are you going with?' 'What time will you be back?' I feel like I'm in a regular *prison*."

Then there's Jeff's mother who says, "I feel left out of Jeff's life. One day my son turns sixteen and we're no longer close—we no longer communicate. If I want to know where he's going, he acts as though I'm trying to control his life. I *am* his mother, after all!"

What's it like at your house? Jeff's mother wants to be his friend as well as his mother. Jeff just wants to go his way and be left alone. "If she was a friend, she wouldn't bug me all the time," he complains.

Humble yourselves under the mighty hand of God, that he may exalt you in due time: casting all your care upon him; for he careth for you.
1 Peter 5:6, 7, KJV

154

Jeff's mother told me she'd be happy if Jeff just "communicated" once in a while. What is your definition of communicating? (Girls think a little differently than guys do about communicating, you know. Girls find the language of emotions easier to speak than guys do. Guys often prefer to speak a language of facts. A happy relationship is when both languages are spoken and you're able to communicate your feelings, thoughts, ideas, goals, as well as your knowledge of sports, politics, art or nuclear physics.)

Jeff told me he'd be happy if his parents didn't "grill" him every day. He felt his life was his business, and besides, his parents were totally uncool about things.

So what should Jeff do? How can Jeff's parents be convinced that he is actually a real person with real feelings and thoughts—and that he doesn't want to talk about things he isn't sure about?

Usually if you're going somewhere the Lord approves of, you don't have to be afraid to say it. The first question to ask yourself is, "What if Jesus was asking me where I'm going, whom I'm going with, and when I'll be home? Could I tell Him? Would He approve and be glad He was going along with me?"

If Jesus approves, you can tell your parents. It's called "communicating"—and parents like that, believe me.

Here are five simple steps to have peace in your house. Follow these and you'll experience results nothing short of miraculous, *and* you'll develop new communicating skills that could last you a lifetime.

Wonder Tips for a Teenager's Happier Home Life

1. In the morning, no matter what, even if an earthquake strikes, *always* say loud and clear, "Good morning!" to your parents. Don't say it from the bathroom or the screen door, or waving from the school bus window. Say it eyeball to eyeball, face-to-face to your parental units. This will give the impression that you are a caring person and an integral part of the family.

2. Every time you come home, no matter when, even if

155

you're sleep-walking, *always* say directly to your parental units, "Hi! I'm home!" ("Hi" to siblings is OK, too, but "hi" to parents is a *must*.) If you're home first, *always* say, "*Hi!*" when they walk in the door. Never ever forget to do this. It will bring you hours of joy and peace in your home. You're *communicating*.

3. Develop sentences like the following to say at the dinner table:

> "I'm feeling real good about . . ."
> "The best thing that happened today was . . ."
> "The thing I like best about this family is . . ."
> "The thing I like best about my school is . . ."

Even if you don't receive applause for being an open communicator, don't give up. You're giving positive input and you'll reap many rewards for it later on, if not immediately.

4. Whenever your parents ask a question, never ever just answer yes or no. *Always* say something more. If your dad asks, "Did you have a good day in school?" don't just grunt, "Yeah . . ." Say, "Terrific," and then add, "I got an *A* on the history test," or "No, not so good," and add, "I was late for first hour and that put me in a bad mood, and I just stayed in a bad mood."

5. Always say "Goodbye" when leaving. Never just run out the door. Your audible "goodbyes" will be received as a caring gesture.

These five *Wonder Tips* will amaze both you and your parental units.

TODAY

Practice your Five Wonder Tips and consider yourself a "communicator"!

*D*ear Lord Jesus, please humble my heart and show me your ways. I take you wherever I go and I ask you to remind me of that. I choose to put you first and that way I won't be ashamed or embarrassed about anything in my life. Help me to be a blessing to my family, especially my parent(s). Open our communication so that we are a strong family unit bonded together in you and your love. Help me to make this happen and be a part of your perfect will. Amen.

Chapter 47

I Am Not Lazy and As Soon As I Get Out of Bed . . .

*D*o people call you lazy? Are you known around the school as "Old Snooze" or "sleepwalking Sue" or just plain "The Zzzz"? Are you a victim of the raging droopies, needful naps, nodding in the shadowy noonness; life in the slo-o-o-o-ow lane?

Are you caught regularly S.I.T.? (Sleeping In Tests) and S.I.L.? (Snoring In Lectures). Are you B.E.? (Bored Easily).

Does your mother complain relentlessly about how you never do anything around the house and she's tired of being your slave, and heaven knows other kids your age do a billion times more work than you do, and how could anybody sleep so much and not be dead?

Have your teachers called the paramedics for you at least twice in the past year?

Then you will have success if you are careful to observe the decrees and laws that the Lord gave Moses for Israel. Be strong and courageous. Do not be afraid or discouraged.

1 Chronicles 22:13

158

If any of the above applies to you, you've got "it." "It" is a very wonderful thing to have. Granted it's a case of gross misunderstanding, but the truth is, the reason you're misunderstood is you're so *creative.*

Creative people need lots of rest.

Your brain needs rest. Your brain is probably the kind that works so intensely each time a really intelligent thought passes through that it wears down quicker than most. That's when you need to hop into bed for a little snooze to refresh yourself.

Now you might find yourself engaging in a needful little snooze during Library, Study Hall, English, Math, Physics, Geometry, History or Science—but do try to remember not to fall asleep during lunch because that would be rude.

There is a condition, however. If you are going to take seriously Psalm 127:2 ("He gives his beloved sleep"), you must remember the words in our verse for today: "Be strong and courageous. Do not be afraid or discouraged."

Sleep can be an escape from problems. It's not escape you need, it's *courage.* It's not numbness you crave, it's *strength.* When trials come your way and when it looks like it's going to start raining troubles, get creative! *Do something!*

Some of those old misbeliefs that could be playing with your mind:

People should always treat me exactly as I want.

I should never lose anything.

I should always be perfect and so should everybody else.

Do a little check-up now:

When you tell yourself:	*Do you counter with the truth such as?—*
1. I should get what I want.	1. If I don't get what I want, it's not the end of the world.

2. Nobody should criticize me.	2. It's not the greatest to be criticized, but I can accept it as constructive. I can use it to be creative. I am OK!
3. Nobody else's feelings are as important as mine.	3. My feelings are no less and no more important than anybody else's.
4. I shouldn't have to suffer.	4. I am strong and courageous. I am not afraid or discouraged.

TODAY

Be creative. God gives success to those who obey Him and walk in His ways. His ways always include courage and strength. Not your strength, but His strength in you. Take it.

In the name of Jesus, I choose to make my problems a creative challenge. I will create excitement, enthusiasm and interests in my life. I choose God's success. Thank you, Lord, for rest, and thank you, Lord, for courage and strength. Amen.

Chapter 48

To Be or Not to Be

The air around you is flaming hot with frustration. Disappointment fills every corner. You tell yourself, *Everything happens to me! This is the worst day of my entire life!* And so was yesterday, you remind yourself. Will your misery never end? Where's that happy Christian life you've heard so much about?

"Nobody cares about *me*," you tell your dog. "I might as well roll over and just *die*." He wags his tail and gives you a doggy grin. (It's useless to tell the dog you're thinking of ending it all. You always want to tell a *person* so you'll get some attention. "I'm going to the river, Mom" might raise an eyebrow or two.)

You deserve respect, attention, concern and love. You deserve to be cherished, encour-

The Lord upholds all those who fall and lifts up all who are bowed down.
Psalm 145:14

aged, blessed and admired. But threatening suicide won't make you feel terrific. Doing yourself in won't get you what you really want.

People who threaten suicide are not actually wanting to die—they want to end their pain. And because they are uninformed and do not know of alternative measures to take, they sometimes do actually succeed in taking their lives. Studies show that suicide victims are often angry people who take out their anger on the world by a violent and hostile act against their own lives.

The Word of God tells us, "My people are destroyed from lack of knowledge" (Hosea 4:6). When you feel the most hopeless it's when you know the least about the personality of God. When you feel terrible about yourself and the world around you, you're not in tune with the song in God's heart. You need a good dose of Psalm 68:19: "Praise be to the Lord, to God our Savior, who daily bears our burdens." You need a long drink of Psalm 68:20: "Our God is a God who saves; from the Sovereign Lord comes escape from death."

Life is very disappointing at times. People are disappointing at times. The world can be a pretty rotten place at times. Your feelings of frustration, hopelessness, and being bummed out are controllable. Yes, controllable. You can teach yourself to be bummed out or not to be bummed out. You can choose your feelings. God isn't wringing His hands in despair.

God is saying to you today, "Do not fear, for I am with you; do not be dismayed, for I am your God. I will strengthen you and help you; I will uphold you with my righteous right hand" (Isaiah 41:10).

Here's what to tell yourself when you think there's no way out of your troubles:

1. Tell yourself, "I am disappointed and hurt, but it won't last. Things change. Jesus makes things better. I won't be in this situation forever."
2. I make things happen because Jesus is my strength

163

and my salvation. I can make depression happen and I make gladness happen. I choose my feelings."

3. "When I feel disappointed and hopeless, it isn't the end of the world. I can go on with my life in a positive way. I can choose constructive rewards and good things to help myself feel better."

4. "The Lord Jesus answers my prayers. The Lord Jesus loves me. The Lord Jesus cares and watches my every move. He is with me now. He holds me up when I'm hurt and disappointed. He understands my frustration and my feelings of hopelessness. He never leaves or forsakes me. I give this situation entirely to Him right now."

TODAY

Look up and memorize these scripture verses—Isaiah 40:31 and Proverbs 12:19.

Even though I get discouraged at times, Lord Jesus, I know you are here with me. I alone choose my feelings and I am asking you to remind me of that. The truth lasts forever and I am choosing now to believe and act on the truth of your Word. My life is precious and I am special to you. Thank you, Lord Jesus. I love you and worship you. I'll live for you. Amen.

Chapter 49

Beyond Yourself

The seven children of the Schaeffer family range from two-years-old to sixteen. The Schaeffers are one of the fast-growing number of families choosing home school over public or private schools.

Every day the Schaeffer children study and work hard at their studies, but they learn at home in the Christian atmosphere their parents provide. The primary teacher is their mother.

The Schaeffers have been very happy with home school. Buddy is the sixteen-year-old. Last year he began having doubts about home school and himself. He was afraid that he was "different" from other kids. He worried about not being accepted by kids his age who went to public or private schools.

. . . those who live in accordance with the Spirit have their minds set on what the Spirit desires.
Romans 8:5b

165

Buddy's worries were unfounded though. Others liked him not for the school he attends, but for the kind of person he is.

Buddy is fun and likeable. People say he is the kind of person you want to get to know and have as a friend. His pastor thinks Buddy will be a leader some day. But Buddy hasn't seen himself in such positive terms. Last year he felt too intimidated to try out for his church's Christmas musical-drama. Buddy had dreamed of being a part of it. Faced again with the opportunity, he tried to talk himself out of auditioning.

He was telling himself, "I can't do this. This is dumb of me to try. I'm making a fool out of myself."

The Lord didn't see Buddy as making a fool out of himself. The Lord saw Buddy as courageous and filled with His Spirit. Buddy was so locked in his own self-absorption that he couldn't see beyond himself.

Can you identify with Buddy? He landed a small part in the Christmas play that year and this year he's playing one of the leads. Looking back now, he sees that his feelings of inferiority all stemmed from not seeing himself as the Lord saw him. The Lord never wants you to be a hopeless failure or unliked or untalented, or any other horrible thing you can think about yourself.

Buddy has lots of friends his age from church and he plays on a YMCA soccer team besides the church softball team. In two years he'll be ready for college.

God created you to allow His Spirit to dominate your life. The things you want are important to Him. He wants you to see beyond yourself and into His mind and heart.

TODAY

Choose to see yourself as a person greatly cherished by God and walking in His Spirit. He has told you that when your ways please Him, He makes even your enemies to be at peace with you (Prov. 16:7).

Dear Lord Jesus, thank you for making me likeable and acceptable no matter where I live, where I go to school or what I look like. Thank you for giving me confidence in you and your love for me.

Chapter 50

Did You Hear About. . . ?

When it came to gossip at my high school, we were unbeatable. You could walk down any corridor at any time of day and get an earful about almost anybody. Not known for our football team or our debating team, our gossip team really excelled.

One day I thought up a pact to present to my girlfriends. "Let's promise not to talk bad about each other ever!" was my modest proposal. The reaction was one of stunned silence. They looked at me as though I had just dropped out of a tall tree in search of bananas.

So I revised the proposal. "How about we promise not to say anything bad about each other for just this year?"

"Define 'say anything bad,'" one friend said somberly.

My mouth will speak
words of wisdom . . .
                Psalm 49:3

"Gossip!" I answered. "Just plain *gossip*. Let's not do it—I mean, let's try not to talk bad about each other—"

I could see their eyes clouding over in confusion. "Let's say only *good* things, can you picture it?" I smiled weakly and waited.

I could tell they thought I was on one of my IMPROVE THE WORLD plights. "For a *whole year*? Are you serious? Who's to say what is gossip and what isn't?" one of the girls grumbled.

"We *all* know what gossip is. It's saying unkind things about somebody else. It's telling lies, it's talking behind someone's back, it's hurtful and damaging. And it makes enemies out friends." I wasn't sure if I was getting through.

I suggested we try my idea for six months—one month—finally, we settled for one day. Saturday. I'll never forget it. It was one of the worst days in my life. The phone didn't ring once for me. Not one friend dropped by. I sat alone in my room with a gray cloud of doom over my head.

My mother came in and sat down beside me. "Mom," I blurted tragically, "I haven't got a soul on this earth to talk to except you. We girls made a pact not to gossip. What's left in life for me now?"

She told me she was proud of me, and then she told me something I'll always remember. "Gossip is like tearing a hole in a feather pillow," she began, "and then shaking that pillow in the wind. The lies are like those feathers, and you can never get them all back. The wind keeps on scattering them."

I knew gossip was wrong. Gossip had hurt each of my friends at one time or another; but although we knew it wasn't right, it seemed almost uncool to stop.

My best friend, LaRee, told me it was easier for her to hate gossip after she had experienced being on the receiving end of it and felt its sting. Maybe that's what it takes for us to start caring about someone else's feelings.

I later learned that gossip doesn't end in high school, or college—it thrives anywhere at any age and it is a male problem as well as a female one. And many Christians are guilty of gossip.

A tenth-grade girl told me recently, tears streaming down her face, how a false rumor about her had been blown into a full-scale scandal. The girl was horrified at the story, but by the time she heard it the damage was done. She couldn't track down every person who had listened to the gossip and tell them the truth. She couldn't place an ad in the newspaper explaining herself to everyone in town. It was too late. The feathers were scattered too far.

The Bible says, "He who guards his lips guards his soul" (Prov. 13:3). *The only way to defeat gossip is to not do it.*

My girlfriends and I learned something from what we called "Black Saturday." We learned how easy it was to be unkind without even realizing it. We learned how much more trust and genuine friendship we had without gossip. And the life-changing effect it had on me was to promise the Lord to "guard" my mouth. I didn't want my life to be a scatterer of feathers.

TODMY

Even if you hear stories about someone else, or if you don't happen to like someone, be sure to keep a guard over your mouth. Don't utter one syllable of gossip.

Dear Jesus, I am choosing now to keep guard over my mouth. I don't want to be on the receiving end of gossip and I don't want to dish it out either. You have told us that a wise person stores up godly wisdom but the mouth of a fool invites ruin (Prov. 10:14). You taught us to love one another. Oh Lord, help me to hate gossip. Amen.

Chapter 51

You're on the Witness Stand

*I*magine yourself on trial. It's a serious offense, they say. You're scared. I'm scared. Here comes the judge. "Don't mumble," your mother says as your name is called. Suddenly you're on the stand, you've taken the oath, and the Prosecuting Attorney (PA) approaches ominously.

    PA: Your name?

YOU: Mumble. Mumble.

    PA: (Confused) What was that? Thaddeus Wshllebvbee?

YOU: (Mumbling louder in a correcting tone of voice) Mumble! Mumble!

    PA: (Sighing) Oh well, it doesn't matter.

YOU: Mumble! Mumble! (You're indignant. Sounds like you're saying it matters to you—)

    PA: We'd like to get on with the proceedings. Now then, uh, may I call you Defendant X? —

YOU: *Mumble! Mumble!* (Sounds like, "Do what you want, you fat frog," but it's hard to tell.)

PA: It's been brought to the attention of this court that you, Defendant X, have been engaging in the illegal use of *thought*.

YOU: (You shrink slightly) Uh . . . (Mumble.)

PA: And that you, Defendant X, have been maliciously ruining your mind, defacing your hopes, dreams and aspirations (You twitch nervously.), that you have been destroying your creativity and clear-headedness. Furthermore, your thoughts have been basically *uncool*!

(Gasps from the court.)

JUDGE: (In disbelief) Do you have anything to say for yourself?

YOU: (Totally zapped) Uh, er . . . (Mumble)

PA: (Pointing a bony finger at your nose) *You*, Defendant X, allegedly, have been *lying* to yourself, *undermining* your potential, making *dumb* assumptions and passing cruel and ungodly judgments on your total *life*. Are these allegations true?

(A hush falls on the court. Sunlight dances on your hair, which only this very morning you hatefully referred to as "tweeked.")

JUDGE: Well? How do you respond to these charges?

(You say nothing. It's absolutely silent as everybody waits for your plea of "guilty" or "not guilty." A mischievous urge to cry out for your old tattered "Blankee" crosses your mind. It's so hard to face the music alone.)

YOU: Uh . . .

JUDGE: (Relentlessly) Is it true the following words have been spoken by you? (Reading) "I'm so stupid!" "I'll never pass this class!" "I can't do anything right!" "When I'm dead everybody will be sorry!" "Other people are better off than me!" "Everybody hates me!" "I'm so

172

ugly!" "Everything bad happens to me!"

    (The court goes bonkers. A lady in the back row wearing an "I-heart-guppies" T-shirt dissolves in sobs.)

YOU: (Digging your toe in the floor) Dah . . . er, uh . . . (Your friends are totally embarrassed.)

JUDGE: Well?

PA: Well?

COURT: *Well?*

YOU: Yes. I said those things.

JUDGE: You actually said, "I'm so stupid" out *loud?*

YOU: Yes.

    (Three people faint in shock. The judge pales. The prosecuting attorney licks his chops, smooths his mustache, clicks his teeth. You're just another chump to haul off to the clinker. Your attorney is in tears.)

YOU: I know I said those things, and worse things than these that have been cited. I even said, "I want to die young" and "I hate the whole world."

    (Your mother waves your lunch bag collection at the judge, shouting, "Temporary insanity runs in the family! He's not responsible for his words!" Somebody else yells, "We are *all* responsible for our actions and our words! Your Honor, this woman is aiding and abetting a criminal!")

JUDGE: (Red-faced, flustered and breathless) Order!

YOU: Your honor, it's true—I have said those things. Once I said, "It's not my fault that I'm the way I am."

PA: Correction. You said it twice.

MOTHER: Correction, correction. He says it all the time.

YOU: You're right, Mom.

PA: It sounds to me like this mother *and* offspring ought to be on trial. Not taking responsibility

173

for their own thoughts and words!

YOU: I am the guilty one! I'm guilty, guilty, *guilty!*
(Hysteria breaks out in the court. People are jumping up and down, stamping their feet, sobbing, angry, hurt, outraged.)

PA: (Screaming above the roar of the crowd) I think we've heard enough here. By Defendant X's own admission of guilt, there can be only one verdict, *guilty.*

COURT: And the maximum sentence!

JUDGE: Everybody wants the maximum sentence. It's the best thing that could happen to anybody.
(The court is still frenzied. Several people are weeping out of heartfelt compassion for your lost and fallen mind. A panhandler runs up to you and offers you a dime. The jury screams, "Guilty!")

JUDGE: (Finally gaining order in the court) I sentence YOU, Defendent X, to serve the maximum sentence of 99 years—
(The court goes wild. Pandemonium breaks loose. Cheering, throwing hats in the air, Bibles are held up triumphantly.)

JUDGE: (Continuing) The maximum sentence of 99 years of *telling yourself the truth!*

YOU: (Grinning through tears) Thank you, Your Honor—

JUDGE: And that's not all! I also sentence you to daily telling your mother the truth, which is, "I am responsible for my actions and especially for my thoughts." You will hereby allow only those thoughts in your mind which are compatible with the Word of God.
(Much cheering and celebrating. People are hugging and inviting each other over for lunch. You rush for your mother to find out

174

whatever happened to that old blankee of yours . . .)

Before you leave the court, the judge hands you an additional sheaf of regulations that you will have to observe and report to your "Thought officer," the Holy Spirit, several times a day.

Your regulations include challenging irrational thoughts. You're required to question whether or not there is enough evidence to prove the words you're telling yourself are true or not. (Like, how much evidence do you have that God loves you? And how much evidence do you have that you're going to heaven when you die?)

TODAY

Answer the following questions:

1. Are the words you tell yourself based on *fact* (God's Word) or on false assumption? (Give evidence)

   _____

   _____

2. When you say things like, "It's *terrible*, or *awful* or *the pits*, is it really the worst it can possibly be? Can you give evidence from the Bible that your situation is hopeless?

   _____

   _____

3. Is your thinking getting you what you want?_____

4. Must you always get what you want?

   _____

*F*ather, I am the judge, the prosecuting attorney and the Defendant X in this scenario. I am the only one who can help myself and take the step toward change. I want to have my thoughts under your control. Give me the courage to recognize, admit and challenge my bad thinking. Give me the desire to be open and truthful because you are open and truthful with me. Thank you, Lord.

Your genes aren't faded after all.